MW00398411

The Infinite Pipeline

How to Master Social Media for Business-to-Business Sales Success

BY MIKE ELLSWORTH, ROBBIE JOHNSON, AND KEN MORRIS, JD

Printed in the United States of America

No part of this publication may be reproduced, stored in or introduced into a retrieval system, or transmitted, in any form, or by any means (electronic, mechanical, photocopying, recording, or otherwise), without the prior permission of the publisher. Requests for permission should be directed to **permissions@stratvantage.com**, or mailed to Permissions,

Social Media Performance Group, Inc.,
The Commerce Building, Suite 3101,
8200 Humboldt Avenue So.,
Minneapolis, MN 55431.

Infinite Pipeline™, Social Media Performance Group Community Building Checklist™, Social Media Performance Group™, and the Social Media Performance Group logo are trademarks of Social Media Performance Group, Inc.

www.SocialMediaPerformanceGroup.com

ISBN-13: 978-0-9884682-0-7

Table of Contents

Table of Figures

How to Read this Book

There are two Infinite Pipeline books, each for a different audience. This book is for sales people. It contains everything you need to get started using social media to sell in business-to-business (B2B) markets.

The other book, *The Infinite Pipeline: How to Master Social Media for Business-to-Business Sales Success, Sales Executive Edition*, is, as you might expect, for sales management.

We make several assumptions in this book, the first of which is that sales people, as a whole, would rather do than read. Robbie is fond of joking that all sales people have ADD, RLS and Tourette's. If that's not you, we invite you to read the whole book. But if you're the impatient type, we recommend the must-read sections below.

We've tried to make the material in this book as action-oriented as possible. However, we've also included some strategy. You can feel free to skip around in the book if you're mostly interested in action items.

The most action-oriented chapters are the *Your First 30, 60, and 90 Days of Social Media* chapters. We don't really recommend you skip right to these chapters because we think understanding a bit more about the Infinite Pipeline concepts is necessary for success in social sales.

So at a minimum, we recommend reading the following chapters and sections:

Chapter or Section	Description
The chapter Why Social Media for Sales? on page 15	A good basis for understanding the power of social media
The sections Welcome Infinite Pipeline™ on page 33 and Perfecting Your Message on page 35	Introductions to Infinite Pipeline and social media messaging
The chapter Infinite Pipeline™ Concepts Explained on page 53	A basic grounding in the Infinite Pipeline system

The chapter Be Careful Out There! on page 83	Warnings on the potential consequences of misusing social media
The chapters: • Your First 30 Days on Social Media on page 109 • Your First 60 Days on Social Media on page 129 • Your First 90 Days on Social Media on page 159	Extensive how-to instructions on how to engage in Infinite Pipeline social selling

We've also helped you decide what parts of this book to read by including *Where to Go Next* sections at the end of some chapters.

Some of the concepts in the Infinite Pipeline Sales Development Process require sales management and other areas of your company in order to implement. As a sales person, you may not be able to take advantage of these concepts buy yourself. However, many of the community concepts can prove valuable in helping you change your thinking about that huge list of contacts you have. Where possible, we suggest ways a lone sales person can benefit from the Infinite Pipeline concepts that might seem beyond your grasp.

However you read this book, we hope you find the concepts it contains sensible but challenging, and ultimately useful.

Mike Ellsworth
Robbie Johnson
Ken Morris, JD

Why Social Media for Sales?

It used to be a truism that if a salesperson made 100 cold calls, he or she would get 10 appointments, and out of those ten appointments, one sale. Entire industries, particularly insurance and financial services companies, have been built around this strategy. However, the end result of making 100 cold calls today is leaving 100 voicemails that are ignored by 100 prospects.

Koka Sexton
Inbound Marketing Manager
InsideView

One of the Social Media Performance Group partners used to work for a $4 million IT consulting company. He called up a major multibillion dollar international company and inquired about getting on their vendor list.

The purchasing guy actually laughed at the request. "We just sliced our vendor list in half to get rid of little companies like yours. You have no chance," the guy said.

Robbie was not to be dissuaded. He searched on LinkedIn and found several company employees to target. Since group memberships are often listed on people's profiles, he found and joined the groups they belonged to. If they contributed something to the group, he messaged them to ask a question about it, and otherwise found excuses to engage with them.

He did no selling; he asked them about their challenges, offered interesting information, advice and links, and eventually it was time to ask them to connect, and later, to have coffee.

After nine months of cultivating these relationships, one of his contacts (who was not someone you would ordinarily target as a decision-maker) said, "Hey, we've got a new project starting that you guys would be perfect for. I'll have the purchasing guy give you a call."

And who eventually called him? You got it: the laugher. Robbie's company got the $500K contract, and got on the vendor list of this huge company.

He never once pitched any of his LinkedIn contacts.

Let's repeat: Robbie **never once** pitched a decision-maker. He never once did the smiling and dialing thing. He never once filled up prospects' voice mail with requests for their time.

He just used social media.

Or more accurately, he just used this new tool to do something good sales people do instinctively using other means: build relationships. Connecting on social media is not about selling yourself, but rather about building over time a mutually beneficial relationship based on trust.

How Many Dials?

When Robbie's old-style sales manager hired him he asked the standard question, "How many dials will you do a day?" Robbie answered, "None."

Dumbfounded, the manager repeated, "None?"

"That's right," Robbie said, "I'm going to do it all with social media."

"But how am I going to measure you?" came the inevitable response.

"How about by results?" Robbie replied.

Needless to say, it took a sales job to get his manager to agree to a trial of this new way to close sales. And over the next nine months, not only did Robbie close the giant corporation, he also closed four other large organizations and started more than a half dozen strategic partnerships — all with no smiling and dialing.

The Failure of Traditional Sales Metrics

This was not the first time Robbie was challenged for not meeting traditional sales metrics. While he was selling for a large enterprise software company, Robbie's manager called him into his office.

"Robbie, I don't quite know how to bring this up," the man said.

"What is it," asked Robbie. "We both know I'm 4X quota for this quarter."

"That's just it," his manager said. "I'm very pleased. But I'm getting flack from above because, well, your metrics suck. You're going to have to up your number of dials."

"You've got to be kidding," Robbie said. The manager assured him it was out of his hands.

So Robbie figured out how to dial all his outgoing lines at once and hang up once he inevitably reached prospects' voice mail (sound familiar?). He got his number of dials up to the minimum, and the organization left him alone. Until one day, his manager called him back into his office.

"OK, Robbie, I noticed in the logs that you got 30 calls done in 10 minutes. I figured out how you're doing all those dials, and, frankly, I couldn't care less because you're still way over quota. But some of the other guys have caught on and now my boss wants us to do something about this dialing technique of yours."

"Sorry, boss," was all Robbie could say.

The Challenge of Smiling and Dialing

Sales expert and best-selling author Jill Konrath says that in order to reach what she calls "crazy-busy" prospects, the old sales paradigm must change.[1]

> In the new sales climate, focusing on your FABs (features-advantages-benefits) creates insurmountable obstacles. Using clever objection-handling techniques insults your prospect's intelligence.
>
> And employing "always be closing" tactics is the surest way to prematurely end potentially fruitful relationships.
>
> Today YOU are the primary differentiator, not your product or service. That means you need to be at the top of your game all the time—or you'll get deleted, delayed or dismissed entirely.

To succeed today, **you** need to become an invaluable resource.

You need to know your prospect better and tailor your solutions to their problems. You may think that's the "same as it ever was" but with today's access to information, your prospect is looking for more than basic information about what you're selling.

They're looking for recommendations from your customers; they're looking at what your haters are saying about you; and they couldn't care less about your brochureware.

To succeed in the new marketplace, you need to add value during the sales process. And you need to develop your own personal brand so that when customers or prospects have a problem, you come instantly to mind as the solution.

How can you add value? One way is by helping your customers and prospects think through how they'll use your product. To do this, you'll provide perspective in addition to product information. The best way to do this is to place yourself in your prospect's shoes. Imagine what they would want out of your product or from a connection with you and try to deliver on that.

---

1 Jill Konrath's *SNAP Selling: Speed Up Sales and Win More Business with Today's Frazzled Customers*: amzn.to/nrNZzt

Sales Training Connection puts it this way: "For example, through a conversation a buyer might realize that he hadn't thought of the implications of rolling out a solution in Europe or she underestimated the impact on other divisions."[2]

Traditional Sales Approaches Must Change

Konrath isn't the only sales strategist warning about the increasing problems of getting the attention of clients and prospects. Geoffrey James, blogging on BNET, said:

> Social media has become massively more important because customers have stopped listening to vendors and analyst/reviewers. Think about that. Most of your marketing and analyst relations and press relations are being trumped by customers talking to customers.

Market researcher Forrester concurs and describes the evolving role of marketing in sales:

> Marketing now owns most of the buying cycle. In the age of the customer, social technology empowers customers with extensive information about your company and products.

> Buyers now put off talking with salespeople until they are ready for price quotes, which means marketing now owns a much bigger piece of the lead-to-revenue cycle. Marketers must nurture prospects for months or years before they turn into sales opportunities, so it is critical to know how you are performing at each interim stage a buyer goes through.

And yet, are these marketing departments equipped for this task? Another Forrester finding casts some doubt:

> When asked to name the five biggest weaknesses of their marketing department, 49 percent of marketing leaders cited "use of analytics to guide marketing decisions," second only to "mastery of social media tools."[3]

2 Sales Training Connection's *Should sales people leverage the power of branding to differentiate themselves?* bit.ly/zl9DJC
3 Forrester's *Metrics That Matter For B2B Marketers: Revenue Impact Should Top The CMO's Management Dashboard:* bit.ly/yGyHO8

What You Know About Who You Know

So you might be thinking: "You're telling me everything I know about sales is wrong!"

Nothing could be further from the truth.

Yes, it's true (and if you think about it, you know this) that some of your sales tactics don't work as well as they used to.

Yes it's true that to succeed, you're going to need to use some new tactics.

But what you've always known about sales — people often buy because of the relationship you've established with them — is still true, and will probably always be. So if you've mastered the art of the relationship sell, you're perfectly positioned to use a new tool — social media — to find, contact, begin, and nurture relationships with your prospects.

InsideView has this to say about dealing with customers in this new environment of easy access to information:

> While sales may always remain a relationship-driven business, the power of just "who you know" is already being trumped by "what you know about who you know."[4]

What you know about who you know gives you new ways to reach out to prospects and form connections. So you have the phone number of the decision-maker. Big deal. You'll never get him or her on the phone, and if you do, they likely won't have the time to listen to your pitch. But knowing the decision-maker loves line dancing or bass fishing or Duke basketball can help you engage with them in a low-pressure way, and help you build a trust relationship.

To combat the fact that prospects now have lots of ways to find out about you — and your competition — you're going to need some new tactics, and social media is a powerful tool that just might help.

A quote from a C-level respondent to a 2009 study from Business.com puts it all into focus:

> On Twitter, the people I follow provide me with more relevant links and information than any other tool. It saves me time and helps me learn about new technologies or innovative ideas, as they are happening.[5]

---

4 InsideView's *How to Sell to Customer 2.0* bit.ly/rhVKxZ
5 Business.com's *Engaging Small Business Decision Makers Through Social Media*: bit.ly/upLFDn

You're reading this book because you're at least curious about social media. You probably want to know why there's such a fuss about it, and you'd like to find out if it can help your sales efforts. We'll get to all these topics, but first, let's talk about why you should care at all about social media.

Why You Should Care about Social Media

We've given you a little introduction to the way things are changing for sales, and we've asserted that sales people who know how to create relationships are the ones likely to achieve sales success in the new environment. Let's take just a moment to take a deeper look at why things have changed.

Why did it get so hard close prospects? After all, with the Web, it's insanely easy to find new prospects. If you know how to use Google, you can easily find the customers or the companies in your category. With a little work, you can find the names, email addresses, and even the phone numbers of those prospects so you can begin smiling and dialing.

That's the problem.

Every other sales person in your category has the same advantage. And they are bombarding the poor prospects with emails, dials, direct mail, TV and radio ads, billboards, and on and on.

The Internet has leveled the playing field by making it extremely easy to annoy prospects.

Robbie tells a story about when he used to sell for that large enterprise software company we mentioned previously, which we'll call BigB2B. He and his sales manager were calling on the CIO of a large client; let's call him Jim. After they were ushered into Jim's office, he says, "Hold on a second. I want to check my voice messages." Robbie and his manager exchange a glance that says, "That's odd."

The guy punches up his voice mail and puts it on speaker. He plays the first message: "Hi, I'm John Smith from BigB2B, I'd like to talk to you…" The CIO stabs the button to play the next message: "Hi, this is Mary Doe from BigB2B. I'd like to talk to you about…" Again and again Jim plays similar messages, about a dozen or so.

"Make … it … stop!" Jim says. "I get these all the time. I'm a big customer of yours but you keep pestering me with these smiling and dialing dopes. Make it stop or I'm likely to go to your competitors just for peace of mind."

Robbie and his manager slunk out of the office, realizing they needed to change their approach. Jim was a good client, and they had a good relationship with him. But the relationship was jeopardized by ineffective, old-style sales techniques.

Social Media Changes the Game

What has driven the changes in the B2B sales process? SiriusDecisions reports[6] that the average B2B buyer is 70 percent of the way through their buying process before ever speaking to a sales rep.

See why they don't need you and your sales brochures and your slide deck? They've got the basic info. They want to know your differentiation.

In a blog comment, Jill Konrath referred to the changed role of the sales person: [7]

> Where once they were the purveyors of all info related to their offering, they're no longer needed for this purpose. It's all online. Seekers can find detailed coverage of business problems, product evaluations, decision criteria, optimal solutions, etc.

Take a look at some supporting evidence from recent studies: [8]

- In a June 2010 Harris Interactive poll, when asked what sources "influence your decision to use or not use a particular company, brand or product" 71 percent claim reviews from family members or friends exert a "great deal" or "fair amount" of influence.

- ROI Research for Performance found that 53 percent of people on Twitter recommend companies and/or products in their tweets, with 48 percent of them following through on their intention to buy the product.

- In the January 2009 study, "Tech Decision Maker" by Hill & Knowlton, when considering purchases tech decision-makers gave user-generated sites equal importance with traditional media sources. Decision-makers first consider their personal experience (58 percent) when short-listing tech vendors, followed by word-of-mouth and industry analyst reports, tied at 51 percent. Advertising (17 percent) and direct marketing (21 percent) were listed as the least important information sources when short-listing possible vendors.

So the Internet is the problem, right? It makes it easy for your prospects to find out about your products, a role you used to fill. It also makes it easy for sales people to drive your prospects crazy with requests for contact, discussion, and presentations.

6 Reported in Manticore *Technology's New DemandGen Report Survey Reveals Tips for Using Content to Connect with Buyers*: bit.ly/rGiDur
7 Comment on Schulman+Thorogood's *Which came first: Sales 2.0 or Customer 2.0*? bit.ly/pb9LMX
8 Quoted in *Nuanced Media's How Important are Online Customer Reviews?* : bit.ly/uIgULg

While that may be true, the Internet also provides a solution—social media, which provides a new way to facilitate one of the most effective sales techniques out there: creating relationships, person-to-person.

The Rise of Social Media

Social media is the fastest growing segment of the Internet, having recently overtaken online games and email as the most-used category of applications.[9]

Think of how much you use email, and how much those around you use it. People are using social networking more often than they are using email.

In fact, here are some statistics on various social media properties:

• YouTube is now 10 percent of all Internet traffic[1]	• There are 1.5 million blog posts per day (17 per second)[2]
• YouTube & Wikipedia are among the top brands online[3]	• Five of the top 10 Websites are social[4]
• There are more than 144 million blogs[5]	• More than 175,000 new blogs launch every day[6]

Unconvinced? How about a few more statistics?

- If Facebook were a country, it would be the world's third largest,[10] with 900 million people, having overtaken the US, at 308 million[11]

- Nearly two-thirds of US Internet users regularly use a social network (and almost two-thirds of all Americans are on the FTC's no-call list!)[12]

- Nielsen Netview found that in 2010 social media use by Americans dwarfed other online usage by more than two-to-one (see chart below)

---

9 Nielsen Online: bit.ly/bkJZvx
10 For a light-hearted take on what this means, see: bit.ly/alnzw2
11 Facebook's Newsroom: bit.ly/biGYNr
12 Nielsen, Social *Networking's New Global Footprint:* bit.ly/lLH53L and Switched, *FTC's 'Do Not Call' List Hits 200-Million Mark, but Telemarketers Still Call:* aol.it/lqY9Fh

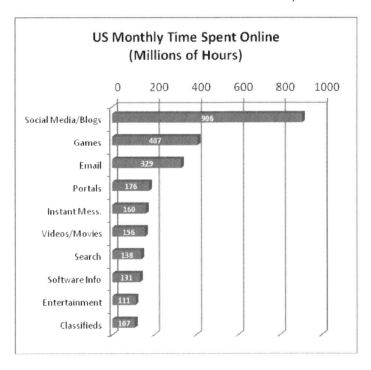

US Monthly Time Spent Online (Millions of Hours)

Social Media/Blogs	906
Games	407
Email	329
Portals	176
Instant Mess.	160
Videos/Movies	156
Search	138
Software Info	131
Entertainment	111
Classifieds	107

Figure 1 — Source: Nielsen Netview, June 2010[13]

But I'm in a B2B Category

A common objection to the use of social media by businesses, and by sales people in particular, is that it is only effective in business-to-consumer (B2C) categories. However, the usage of social media by businesses is even more impressive.

A Forrester Research study found that word of mouth (WOM), which social media enables and accelerates, is the most important influencing factor on business-to-business (B2B) purchase decisions.

---

13 Nielsen Netview: bit.ly/bkJZvx

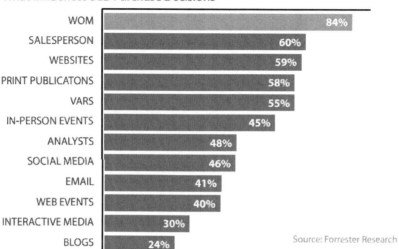

Figure 2 — What Influences B2B Purchase Decisions

Lest you think that B2B buyers aren't present on social media, Forrester has found that they are 20-percent-more-active creators and twice as active on social media as consumers.

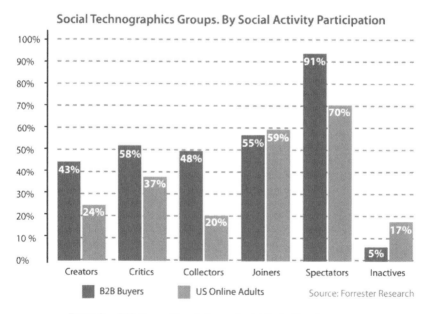

Figure 3 — B2B Buyers More Active on Social Media than Consumers

Managed security company Network Box found in a January, 2011 report[14] that social media sites dominate Internet usage by businesses. According to the company, employees using Facebook and YouTube accounted for 16 percent of all corporate bandwidth during 2010.

An April, 2011 study by BtoB Magazine found that 93 percent of B2B marketers use some form of social media marketing, with most focusing on the most popular channels (LinkedIn, Facebook and Twitter).[15]

In fact, Jack Morton Worldwide found that business executives have 118 word of mouth (WOM) conversations per week — compared to 100 for consumers — and are more likely to be brand advocates.

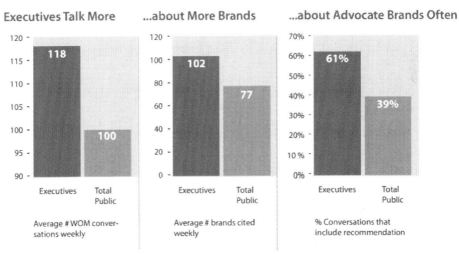

Source: Keller Fay for Jack Morton Worldwide.

Figure 4 — Business Executives Have More Word of Mouth Conversations than Consumers

For those who believe that social media can't be measured or show ROI, Zuberance[16] is among several companies who would beg to differ. By tracking open rates on email, click-through rates on Websites, and conversions to sales, online WOM and social media activity can be tracked closely.

14 Network Box press release, *7.9 per cent of all business internet traffic goes to Facebook in 2010, revealed by Network Box bandwidth usage survey* : bit.ly/PgpMNv
15 BtoB magazine's *Emerging Trends in B2B Social Media Marketing* bit.ly/oOjRBR
16 Zuberance's *Three Surprising Facts About Brand Advocates*: bit.ly/OljJVI

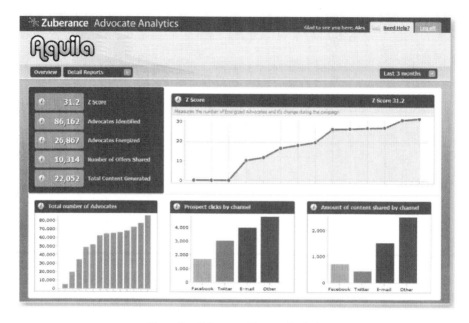

Figure 5 — Zuberance Advocate Analysis

A brand advocate (a type of person we prefer to call an evangelist) is someone who passionately recommends a company or its products. As the number of brand advocates grow, so does the content they generate, which means more recommendations for your products. And advocates are active in B2B categories as well, as the next figure demonstrates:

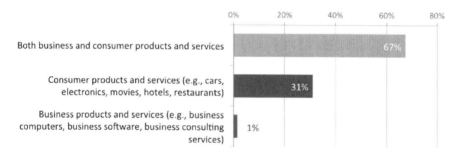

Figure 6 — Types of Brand Advocate Recommendations

And if all that doesn't do it for you, consider the fact that Amazon recently was granted a patent[17] for "A networked computer system [that] provides various services for assisting users in locating, and establishing contact relationships with, other users," — in other words, social networking. When the big boys get this serious, you know something's going on.

We'll show you lots of other good reasons to be interested in social media throughout this book.

---

17 Amazon granted a social networking patent: bit.ly/cyB3p8

Today's Sales Challenges

We market and sell in a brave new world where prospects are equipped with near X-ray vision into companies, products and people they are considering doing business with.

Pelin Wood Thorogood
Schulman+Thorogood

We've already talked a bit about the challenges you're facing these days. Many sales strategists agree that the sales process is overdue for an evolution, from Sales 1.0 to Sales 2.0, which embraces various new tools, information sources, and organizational changes to enable sales people to improve results.

Sales 1.0

Pretty much all the techniques you're using to sell today were invented and perfected in the 1890s. Think about that for a second.

Is it possible that there's been nothing truly new in sales techniques in the last 120 years?

Well, take a look at the sales concepts the founder of National Cash Register, John Patterson, developed way back then:

- Territories
- Prospecting scripts
- Sales conventions
- Thematic sales contests
- Quotas
- Direct mail and the reply card
- The President's Club

One of Patterson's salesmen described his sales process, and it's quite relevant to both Sales 1.0 and Sales 2.0:

> My method of taking orders, I presume, does not vary much from that of other managers. If the party calling is a stranger, the first thing is to learn and know my man, his residence, business, etc., and get his confidence [...][18]

---

18 Harvard Business School, *John H. Patterson and the Sales Strategy of the National Cash Register Company, 1884 to 1922*: bit.ly/v9Gsgw

For sure, this component of the B2B sales method hasn't changed, and doesn't fundamentally change in Sales 2.0.

Sales 2.0

The term "Sales 2.0" was coined by Nigel Edelshain, CEO of Sales 2.0, LLC, in 2006. While exact definitions of the term vary, most include the use of new electronic tools such as Customer Relationship Management (CRM) systems as well as a closer integration of sales and marketing processes.

Christian Smagg, Marketing Director - Communications, Media & Technology at Accenture, offered this definition in a LinkedIn answer:[19]

> Sales 2.0 should be considered as the synthesis of new technologies, models, processes and mindsets. It is about leveraging people, process, technology, and knowledge to make significant gains. It means integrating the power of Web 2.0 and on-demand technologies with proven sales techniques to increase sales velocity and volume. It also relates to increased communication and collaboration between sellers and buyers and within the selling team, together with a proactive and visible integration of knowledge and measurement of the buying cycle into the sales cycle.

Beyond Sales 2.0

If you ask many sales people about the success of Sales 2.0, you may find that they don't feel it lived up to its promise. In many ways, Sales 2.0 turned into Big Brother: another, more intrusive way to keep tabs on sales people; a more precise way to count dials. In fact, Sales 2.0 as practiced by many companies is just 1.0 digitized.

This was driven home to Robbie in a recent incident. His company had a state-of-the-art Web-based CRM system. Like all salespeople at the company, Robbie was supposed to add notes after every contact with a prospect. One day, his boss was asked about a prospect and looked him up in the CRM. He found a record, but no notes. So he assigned a sales person to contact the guy.

The prospect said, in effect, "Why are you calling me? I've been working with Robbie and he's answering a few technical questions before we do the deal." When informed of this wonderful news — an imminent new sale — Robbie's boss hit the roof and called him into his office. "Have you been talking to George Wingnut?" "Sure," said Robbie. "I owe him some hardware requirements and then he's ready to sign."

---

19 LinkedIn Answers: linkd.in/rTToOW

"But," sputtered his boss, "You don't have any notes in the record!" "Right, boss," replied Robbie. "You remember I told you about that trade show last month? I had 30 meetings and talked to at least 100 other prospects. Who has the time to write 130 notes? Either I can nurture the relationship, or document it. Which would you prefer?"

"But if you're hit by a bus, I'm screwed," replied this boss. "I guess so, boss," agreed Robbie.

Sales 2.0, even done properly, no longer fits with the evolution of customers, in our view. Most Sales 2.0 solutions don't fully take into account the effect a tool like social media (often obliquely referred to as Web 2.0) can have on sales results, and how revolutionary its impact can be on the way you build relationships to improve sales results.

With social media, the world is your CRM, and ever-evolving, self-documenting connections are tracked in almost real-time.

Customer 2.0 and You 2.0

You know, it's getting to be quite a fad to name things "2.0."[20] In addition to Sales 2.0, there's Customer 2.0, Business 2.0, Enterprise 2.0, Web 2.0 (which often includes social media), Publishing 2.0, Startup 2.0, even Dating 2.0!

So we'll jump on that bandwagon and talk about You 2.0.

You 2.0 knows how to sell to busy Customer 2.0 by cutting through the noise and getting noticed among the fire-hose torrent of pitches, information, and advertising the average buyer is deluged with.

The You 2.0 sales person knows there is no B2B or B2C. There's just B2P — Business-to-Person, or better yet P2P — Person-to-Person.

Focusing on Person-to-Person selling acknowledges that there are precious few things in this world that aren't bought by people (as opposed to buying by machines, we guess.)

It also means accepting the reality that, for all the similarities, there still are significant differences between B2B customers and B2C customers, especially when it comes to purchasing decision making.

Sure, the B2B buying process is more complicated than B2C, often with layers of management approval required. But everyone involved is a person who has the

---

20 "2.0" Google Search: bit.ly/mTCWPJ

same access to information about you, your products, and your competition as a consumer does.

In fact, the B2B Customer 2.0 has probably long been a B2C Customer 2.0. In a comment on a Schulman+Thorogood blog post, Nigel Edelshain, said:[21]

> Buyers changed their behavior when they got Google. Suddenly they could find all the info they wanted without inviting a sales person into their office for "an update". It only got worse with social media as buyers could talk amongst themselves about products before ever talking to a sales person.
>
> I've seen Sales 2.0 from the outset as sales people using the same kind of tools to "level the playing field".
>
> Today sales people need to be smarter just to get into a buyer's office and start a sales cycle. Things are improving as the tools to help us be smarter have started arriving. Now we just need to use them appropriately and consistently.

Research supports Edelshain's point regarding the effect of the wealth of product information and reviews now available to the average buyer.

A 2011 survey by Lightspeed Research[22] found that only 27 percent of respondents had not conducted online research before buying a product. The majority (62 percent) read reviews online, half (49 percent) researched competitors and half (49 percent) checked price comparison sites.

Despite the differences between B2B and B2C buying, the B2B customer is likely to exhibit the same behavior — exhaustively researching your product before you ever show up at their door.

Pelin Wood Thorogood sums up the evolution of sales and customers this way:[23]

> [...]I think Sales 2.0 is really the sales organization's response to the "evolve or die" mandate they face, given the smarter and more informed buyer they have to sell to: Customer 2.0. I do believe the customer has evolved faster than the sales guy... and I believe this is — at least in part — due to how B2B trends typically follow B2C.

21 Comment on Schulman+Thorogood's *Which came first: Sales 2.0 or Customer 2.0?* **bit.ly/pb9LMX**
22 Lightspeeds' *Consumers Rely on Online Reviews and Price Comparisons to Make Purchase Decisions* **bit.ly/pNnfBP**
23 Schulman+Thorogood's *Which came first: Sales 2.0 or Customer 2.0?* **bit.ly/pb9LMX**

So one of the traditional justifications for a sales call — "Let me update you on our latest offerings" — has essentially disappeared. And Customer 2.0 is far too busy these days to listen to sales pitches. If he or she has a need, they'll become the dreaded Stealth Prospect: They'll research their options on the Web, read reviews from your customers, and ask their peers for their opinions using social networking, all without ever contacting you.

Great. Where does that leave you?

It leaves You 2.0 with a new responsibility: to be where Customer 2.0 is — online, on social media — to hear what they're saying, perfect your message, improve your relationship, and exert your influence there.

Welcome Infinite Pipeline™

We just were talking about You 2.0 and messaging, and we'll get back to that topic in the next section.

But we interrupt that discussion for an important announcement:

Sales 2.0 is dead. Long live Infinite Pipeline!

That's right. We think Sales 2.0 is past its freshness date. Sales 2.0 involved a series of very important shifts in the way you approach your customers and prospects. It added the idea of new tools and automation (like Customer Relationship Management systems). It stressed partnerships with marketing and other company assets. And Sales 2.0 introduced an important concept that Infinite Pipeline builds upon: relationships and communities.

However, the old Sales 2.0 did not take a number of these concepts far enough. Take a look at the following table[24] for a glimpse at what the Infinite Pipeline sales development system (and You 3.0 – you just got a free upgrade!) brings.

---

24 The first two columns are adapted from Intrepid's 2008 white paper, *Sales 2.0: Exploring Paradigm Shifts in Web Technologies, Sales Performance, and Learning* (PDF): **bit.ly/Hw4E0n**

Sales 1.0	Sales 2.0	Infinite Pipeline™
Mass messaging provides sales leads	Semi-personalized messaging provides sales leads	Customers and evangelists provide sales leads
Rigidly following a sales process	Helping prospects buy	Solving prospects' problems
Controlling what the buyer knows	Buyers educate themselves beforehand	Answering buyers' questions
Marketing versus Sales	Integrated & interdependent marketing/sales	Internal sales-oriented community
Selling solutions	Helping customers succeed	Social customer service
High-efficiency versus high-touch	High-efficiency AND high-touch	External customer/ prospect/ evangelist problem-solving community
Volume versus relationships	Relationship-driven volume	Relationship-based problem solving
Salesperson's contacts (relationships) are jealously guarded gold	Salesperson's contacts are shared narrowly via CRM systems	Salesperson's contacts are part of the community
Travel, meeting, schedule hassles	Engaging anytime, anywhere	Always Be Engaging replaces Always Be Closing
Technology is a burden	Technology makes sales reps more effective	Sales reps are immersed in social technology
Count every activity	Measure activities that matter	Measure results
Forecast probability	Forecast predictability	Infinite pipeline
Pipeline volume	Pipeline shape and velocity	Infinite pipeline

Sales 1.0	Sales 2.0	Infinite Pipeline™
Mass prospecting	Networks and communities of unlimited opportunities	Communities that solve problems

There are some big concepts in the Infinite Pipeline column, and we're not going to take them all on right now, but leave them for subsequent chapters. If you're impatient, check out the *Infinite Pipeline™ Concepts Explained* chapter on page 53.

For right now, let's continue our focus on messaging.

Perfecting Your Message

The old media techniques of amping up the volume of marketing messages are becoming increasingly ineffective. Yankelvich Research estimated that many consumers are exposed to 3,000 to 20,000 marketing messages each day.[25] The B2B customer is not only exposed to — and desensitized by — all those messages, but also has to deal with the clutter and annoyance of B2B messages.

Your messages just add to the clutter that busy Customer 2.0 faces.

Later in the book, we lay out a detailed plan for your first 30, 60, and 90 days on social media that goes into greater depth on messaging, but for now, let's talk just a little more about the subject in general.

Stop Pitching to Machines

We know that when you smile and dial, you're most often talking to machines — answering machines or voicemail.

And your typical message may be something like:

> Hi, I'm Joe Doakes with BigB2BCompany and I'd like to talk to you about our new widget/service. I think you'll find our offering is superior to the competition and I'd like to have a moment of your time to update you on our company's offerings. I'd love to share with you the latest industry analyst report that shows our solution to be the best choice to solve your problems. I think we would be a great fit for your company, and I've taken the liberty of sending you some brochures on our solution. So if you get a chance, I'd love to talk with you. You can reach me at . . .

---

25 Quoted in All Points Connect's *Marketing Trends Then vs. Now*: bit.ly/uhR2dg

So what's wrong with this message strategy, which we call *Pleading for a Call Back?*

Well for one, it's too long. Many busy executives will hit the delete button after "with BigB2BCompany" because they're tired of sales people bugging them and offering updates, which they know full well are sales pitches.

Another problem is the message shows no understanding of the executive's business or problems. It's too generic. You are basically asserting that your widget is the solution but you give your prospect no reason to believe that it is.

Additionally, your prospects may not perceive that they have a problem that your solution can solve. This is especially the case if your offering is new for your company or your industry.

Put these various problems together, and we can describe the problem as one of engagement. They're just not that into you. You've given them no reason to engage with you because you haven't attempted to engage them.

Develop Engaging Sales Messages

How about if you tried a different kind of messaging? After all, you're probably still being measured by the old school metric — number of dials — so you might as well work to improve.

Let's take a look at the four problems with typical messaging:

- **Too Long** — Try to keep your voice messages under 30 seconds. You may know this tactic by the term elevator pitch, the amount of information you can impart during a short elevator ride.

- **Lack of Understanding** — Provide a context for your call that indicates you understand the prospect's business and needs

- **Lack of Relevance** — Research your prospect, using traditional and social media means, and identify an actual problem your prospect faces. Figure out a quick way to identify the problem and your solution.

- **Lack of Engagement** — By researching your prospect via social media, find some kind of hook or common interest that the two of you share. It might be a school affiliation, and industry group, or it may even be community-based, like a soccer team your kids are on. Be careful here because you don't want to come off as creepy! Try to work this common interest into your message.

Use Infinite Pipeline Messaging

So what would an Infinite Pipeline conversation with your prospect's voicemail look like? Take a look at these examples and see if you would be more or less likely to return the call.

- **Good** — Hi my name is Jill. When's the last time you looked at the way you're doing your recruiting? I'd love to talk with you about the new ways we can help you do this better.

- **Better** — Hi, my name is Jeff. I'm a fellow alum from XYZ U and it looks like we also share an interest in accounting software. Are you having problems reconciling your receivables? I've got some ideas for a solution, so why don't you give me a call?

- **Best** — Hi, I'm Karen, the ACT! Lady. I've got some ideas for how you can solve the Outlook integration problems that you talked about on the ACT! Software Users group on LinkedIn. Give me a call and I'll share them with you.

So what's going on in these messages?

Stab in the Dark vs. Knowledge about Prospect

In the first message, rather than pitching a solution or just baldly asking for a meeting, Jill may just be taking a stab in the dark that the prospect is struggling with recruiting. Jill might have done some research to determine this, but if so, she could have said "I've heard" rather than asking "are you?"

Jill could have looked up the prospect on LinkedIn and taken a look at his or her stream. That likely would have led to finding the prospect on Facebook or Twitter and more insight into the business problems he or she faces.

Jill's message is obviously an improvement over Joe Doakes' *Pleading for a Call Back*, though.

Random Salesperson vs. Something in Common

In the second message, Jeff immediately tries to establish a rapport with the prospect by citing a common background and interest. We've used this approach to great effect in numerous situations. Many people have deep allegiances to the schools they attended or companies they used to work for. Use LinkedIn and other social media to discover these commonalities and then use them judiciously.

We say judiciously because there's a fine line between being seen as a stalker and being seen as a kindred spirit. For example, Mike once interviewed for a job with a female manager of a huge corporation. He did his research and found out a great deal about the person: the schools she attended, the clubs she belonged to, her hobbies, the name and age and school of her young daughter, what her husband did for a living and where the family lived, even the value of their home!

During the interview, Mike was nervous that he might reveal the depth of his knowledge of the intimate details of her life. Imagine if he blurted out, "So how's Jennifer liking first grade?"

You'll need to feel your way through such conversations, especially considering the growing amount of information, particularly from Facebook, that social media users may not be aware is now public.

Certainly Mike could effectively integrate into the conversation that he also played guitar or loved the Minnesota Timberwolves without revealing that he knew the manager shared his interests.

On the other hand, it is now becoming more common that, when you have your face-to-face meeting with a prospect, they will have checked you out, and may even have seen that you visited their LinkedIn profile.

So doing your social media research and mentioning common interests in your short voicemail is lots better than a canned pitch of any kind.

Semi-Anonymous Salesperson vs. Personal Brand

Karen's message does lots of things right.

She's branded herself as the ACT! Lady. (Karen's a real person, by the way, although we made up the message.)[26] You 3.0 needs to consider creating a similar personal brand.

Let's define personal branding here. We like this general definition of branding by Chris Levkulich of the BrandingBrand blog:[27]

> Branding, in essence, is developing a plan of action that will make your product or company the ONLY solution to its targeted problems.

> Instead of making you stand out among the crowd of other products and having your product being chosen over the competitors as the best product, branding wants to promote the product as **the only product**. Like Kleenex.

---

26   K.J.F. and Associates, Inc. (The Act Lady): linkd.in/Imf8ip
27   Chris Levkulich, BrandingBrand blog: bit.ly/c5o7K0

Wow! Imagine if when people thought about the problem your company solves, they immediately thought of you! What could be better?

In reality, this goal may be unattainable, but that doesn't mean you don't try to develop a personal brand. Here are some points to remember about your personal brand:

- **A brand is a promise** —You need to always deliver on that promise

- **A brand is also a handle** by which people can find you, refer to you, and talk about you online, so make your online presence consistent, including using the same profile picture everywhere

- **If you have a haphazard, disorganized, or confused brand** online, people won't associate what you do with your online presence. This is particularly important if you've got a common name, like **Robbie Johnson.**

- **Be known for something** — If you're just known as the guy who always takes prospects out for expensive dinners, that may get you lots of appointments, but may not deliver many sales. If, instead, you're known as the top thought leader in your industry, or its top problem-solver, wouldn't that be better? Proactively choose what you want to be known for, or the market will choose for you.

Put a slightly different way, here's what your personal brand should do:

- **Inspire Trust**: Everything you do online should build trust

- **Maintain Integrity:** Integrity goes hand-in-hand with trust

- **Build Brand Confidence:** You become the go-to person for your solution

- **Deliver on the Promise:** Your unique selling proposition involves the superior qualities of your product – and you!

We talk about how you can enhance or damage your personal brand in the chapter, *The 10 Commandments of Social Computing* on page 89.

Let's get back to Karen's message.

Karen obviously did her research on her prospect. She looked him or her up on LinkedIn, found the groups he or she participated in and zeroed in on a specific problem — Outlook integration — that she could solve.

Put yourself in the place of the recipient of that voicemail. You've been struggling to solve the problem. Suddenly, someone calls and leaves a message that promises to solve it. How can you not call back?

When Karen accepts the call, her behavior is important. Her brand — the ACT! Lady —promises that she's an expert. She better have the solution. And she should give it to the caller gratis, without pitching.

Does that make you uncomfortable?

You give away your knowledge for free?

Right. Because Karen's after a relationship, not just a sale. She solves your problem. She doesn't subject you to a monologue about how you should hire her, or even a 30-second elevator pitch. She solves your problem.

You naturally are going to be curious. You probably will want to know a bit more about her, and she'll respond to your questions. She won't try to close you. She might mention you can find more ACT! solutions on her Website or that she has a blog where she often posts customer solutions. She might ask for permission to send you a connection request on LinkedIn and to sign you up for her newsletter.

Let's say you thank her and hang up. In a month, when you are having another ACT! problem, who you gonna call?

The ACT! Lady!

Karen has become the go-to resource for your ACT! problems, and the chances are good that she's started a relationship that will deliver sales for her in the future.

We call this the Infinite Pipeline, which involves developing a community full of people who not only know you, know what you can do, but also who will recommend you. We go into lots more detail about the Infinite Pipeline later in the book.

And there's more about building the type of community that sells for you in the next chapter.

Hunt and Kill vs. Farming vs. Infinite Pipeline™

You must get good at one of two things:
planting in the spring
or begging in the fall . . .
A good customer well taken care of
could be more valuable than $10,000 worth of advertising.

Jim Rohn
business philosopher[28]

Some people adopt a take-no-prisoners approach to sales. Often sales organizations codify this into a slogan: You eat what you kill.

We think dead prospects don't buy more than once.

Others subscribe to an approach called farming and this approach is closer to the techniques in the Infinite Pipeline sales development process. Farming involves developing relationships with prospects and cultivating long-term sales.

We think the best sales approach is one in which you never sell.

We said it. You never sell.

Your community sells for you.

Robbie has developed this technique during his years of selling enterprise technology solutions to mid-size and large enterprises. We've transformed this learning into the Infinite Pipeline sales framework and we offer training and consulting for sales forces of all sizes.

Infinite Pipeline involves developing partnerships and relationships to the point where you have tons of referenceable customers, and those customers not only open doors for you, they practically sell the product for you.

---

28 Quotes by Jim Rohn, America's Foremost Business Philosopher, reprinted with permission from Jim Rohn International © 2011

No More Smiling and Dialing

Because he has used social media and the techniques in this book to develop a community of satisfied customers, instead of smiling and dialing, Robbie often receives calls that start like this:

> John Doe and Hugh Bigend say I should call you about your XYZ solution. These guys can't say enough about you and your company. Would you like to talk to me and my team about your solution?

To be honest, these calls don't come in every day, but they do come in.

Far more likely is that Robbie calls a prospect and says (probably to voice mail):

> Jack, I'm Robbie and I've been working with John Doe and Hugh Bigend. They suggested I give you a call and see if we'd be a good fit for your company.

Generally, Robbie will get a call back that goes like this:

> Jack: Robbie, this is Jack Mark returning your call. So you know John and Hugh, huh?

> Robbie: Hi, Jack. Yes, I implemented XYZ solution for John, and we're currently doing an implementation for Hugh at ABC Company.

> Jack: So who are you working with at ABC? [Jack's doing a BS test]

> Robbie: I'm working with Ken, and Bill, and Jay.

> Jack: So you must know Jen and Bonnie? [More BS testing]

> Robbie: Sure, I'm talking to Jen right after this call, in fact.

You get the picture. Jack will hang up and call these various people. They'll give Robbie and his company glowing reviews.

Then, Jack will call Robbie back and set a meeting. He's already predisposed to like what he sees and to buy.

And Robbie did no selling. He just mentioned his references and that they had recommended he call Jack. The references vetted Robbie and his solution and prepared the way for the sale.

Would that be OK with you, if you never did any pitching?

While presenting at a conference, Godard Abel, CEO of BigMachines,[29] once asked, "How many of you have bought from Amazon?" Every one of the 500 attendees raised their hands.

"OK," Abel said, "How many have ever talked to anyone at Amazon?" Two people raised their hands.

So it can be done. Just like Amazon, you can sell without pitching. You just need to build the system that makes it happen.

Sales Systems of the Past

You're undoubtedly familiar with the two main sales systems we mentioned in the beginning of this chapter: Eat What You Kill (EWYK) and farming.

We're not saying that these approaches are obsolete in the evolving sales environment — far from it. Each has its place in our Infinite Pipeline system. Let's take a look at them.

Eat What You Kill

Also called hunting, the Eat What You Kill sales system emphasizes the individual sales person's ability to generate sales transactions and thus get paid. Such schemes benefit the hunter for bringing in new business more than the team that helps sell, process, fulfill, and support the customer. Yet in most B2B sales, it takes more than just the sales person to close the sale. Sales engineers may be needed to demo a technical product and work with the prospect's techies to determine the fit. Other resources may be needed to do assessments of the customer's existing setup to determine how to implement the solution. Fulfillment people may get involved as well as upper sales management. And at the end of the sales process, the whole thing gets dumped in the lap of customer support.

You can see how the reliance on a lone gunman to create sales is somewhat opposed to the idea of social media, which is about establishing lasting relationships. EWYK is generally all about the transaction. Even the metaphor emphasizes the point-in-time transactional nature of the approach: The customer is "killed" and the hunter moves on. The team that supports the sales person gets paid less than the sniper, and that can affect their motivation.

---

29   BigMachines sells online configurators: bit.ly/INYmbm

EWYK may be worse for customers as well, since they are subjected to smiling and dialing, upsells, Always Be Closing, and other annoying techniques employed by hunters.

One example of sales techniques that bug customers is the gang-up sales call: A small army of sales people and their bosses show up, and all of them feel like they've got to get their two cents in during the meeting.

When he was selling Enterprise Resource Planning software (ERP) — which spans several solutions for a company — Robbie often went on sales calls that included:

- Robbie, a sales engineer (SE), and their boss

- The middleware rep, SE, and their boss

- The applications rep, his boss and several SEs representing solutions for:

  » Finance

  » Human resources

  » Supply chain

  » Talent acquisition and so on

- The retail sales rep, boss, and SE

- The Customer Relationship Manager (CRM) rep, enterprise sales rep and their retinues; and on and on

This type of sales call can drive the customer crazy.

Back in the mid-90s Mike went along on a sales call to a company where a friend of his worked. Mike's company hoped to leverage his relationship with his friend, a key decision-maker. In all, there were four people on the sales team — the sales guy, his boss, his boss' boss, and Mike — and as they were all getting seated around the conference table, Mike's friend pulled him aside and said, "OK, I can see I'm in trouble here." "What do you mean?" Mike asked. "You showed up with four people. That means your solution is going to cost $40 grand [lots more money back then than it is now]." "How do you figure that?" asked Mike. "Everybody knows when you guys do a sales call, the price is $10 grand per sales guy." "Hmmm," said Mike. "Well, I don't count; I'm not in sales." But true to Mike's friend's calculation, the solution did turn out to be $40,000.

Whether or not you use the gang-up technique, the sales process can be so harrowing for the customer that, after you close the sale, the customer doesn't want to see you for a long time because the experience was so traumatic. A sales person we know had a customer, who, although they were satisfied and loved the solution, requested that nobody call on them for four months because they couldn't absorb any more. Unfortunately, a month later, a sales rep called the customer up to try to sell the very product they had just bought.

There are multiple problems in the examples we've given, and many of them are related to three aspects of the EWYK or hunter sales technique:

- Managers often don't often trust their hunters to get it right

- Hunters aren't incented to share information with others, possibly resulting in duplicative sales effort

- Customers and prospects are often pelted with so many messages, requests for meetings and other communications that they not only stop listening, but actively avoid any contact

We're not saying, by the way, that you should abandon hunters and the EWYK sales process. Using many of the techniques in this book, you can enable your hunters to work more effectively and solve many or all of the problems we've outlined here. If hunting is working for your organization, you don't need to adopt the entire Infinite Pipeline sales process to benefit from its techniques. However, integrating your hunters into the Infinite Pipeline community can reap tremendous benefits.

Sales Farming

Of the two basic sales techniques we've been talking about, farming for sales is more aligned with social media use than EWYK. The sales farmer builds and cultivates relationships and opportunities, most often within existing accounts. Unlike the hunter, farmers are more likely to thrive as part of a sales team. However, many organizations find that farmers are less likely to turn up new customers since their skill sets are oriented toward deriving maximum value out of existing relationships rather than prospecting.

Since finding new customers is often a lot more expensive than nurturing existing clients, farmers can be an important part of any sales organization.

One problem with the way farmers are currently used is that farmers often don't touch your whole customer base. They may focus on 20 percent of the customers that seem ripe for future sales while the rest of the customers slowly regress to the point that they almost revert to being prospects due to lack of attention.

Your sales organization may be made up of both hunters and farmers. While this arrangement may deliver improved sales versus focusing on either type, customers can dislike being handed off from the big game hunter to the relationship manager and may prefer to deal with a consistent company representative. Of course, in the handoff the company may lose the benefit of previous relationship building.

Lack of a single point of contact can also be a problem for the customer if your company offers several different lines of products.

For example, Mike was a good, referenceable customer for a company that makes Web content management systems (WCMS) that we'll call BigWCMS. He had a great relationship with the sales guy who sold him the software and often got the salesman involved if he had support problems or other roadblocks.

BigWCMS also sells translation and localization software, so when Mike developed a need for machine language translation, he turned to the guy who sold him the WCMS. Unfortunately, the language translation software was handled by a different branch of BigWCMS and after 18 months and a complicated series of meetings and interactions involving several sales people and their bosses, Mike procured a solution.

It turned out, however, that the solution, while feature-rich, did not actually do machine translation, something which the original sales guy was also surprised to find out. After months of struggling with various sales people and managers, Mike finally had to appeal directly to BigWCMS' senior vice president of global sales to get satisfaction.

If this company had had the ability to have a single view of the customer, and the ability to support Mike's need without a cast of thousands getting involved, they wouldn't have risked losing a referenceable client.

Farmers who can help develop a single view of the customer are an important component of the Infinite Pipeline approach, which gives them more tools and more support to ensure customer satisfaction.

Eat What You Kill vs. Infinite Pipeline

We've briefly outlined some of the limitations of the EWYK technique. We obviously think that, especially in B2B sales, relationships are important and hunters aren't generally incented to maintain a relationship; many regard it as the necessary overhead of the hunt. While hunters will maintain contact by periodically touching base with customers, they are generally transaction-oriented and more interested in the thrill of the hunt and getting that sale than in relationship nurturing.

Infinite Pipeline involves building a community of customers and prospects that can generate leads and new business through collaboration and connectedness. As a refresher, here are the characteristics of the Infinite Pipeline sales development process we laid out in the previous chapter:

Customers and evangelists provide sales leads	Solving prospects' problems	Answering buyers' questions
Internal sales-oriented community	Social customer service	External customer/ prospect/ evangelist community
Relationship-based problem solving	Salesperson's contacts are part of the community	Always Be Engaging replaces Always Be Closing

We'll get into lots more detail in later sections, but for now, let's take a look at the differences between eat what you kill and Infinite Pipeline.

Eat What You Kill	Infinite Pipeline™
You're on your own – anyone helping is after a slice	You're part of a team that's building a community
Marketing, support or anything post-sales is a distraction	Customer care drives customer satisfaction drives sales
"They're my contacts"	They're part of the community
You take all the risk – if the pipeline dries up, you're out of a job	It's everyone's responsibility to grow business from existing community members — prospects as well as current customers

Eat What You Kill	Infinite Pipeline™
Your personal brand is paramount	Your customer is paramount
You're on a draw until you can book sufficient business	The whole sales team is compensated for managing profitable customer relationships
You care about the deal, not the profit	Everyone manages the profitability of customers
Business development is a waste of time; you're a sales person	Business development is what everyone does
You depend upon a certain ignorance in your customers	Everyone educates customers about issues, trends, products and services
If the customer buys something that's not a fit, it's not your fault	Ensuring solutions fit the customer is everyone's job
A sale is a one-time thing, and then you're on to the next	A sale is either the beginning or the continuation of a relationship that is likely to produce more sales
Marketing goes their way; you go your way	Marketing and Sales understand customer needs and collaborate on products

Traditional Farming vs. Infinite Pipeline Farming

As we've said, traditional Farmers have an orientation and skill set that is very transferable into the Infinite Pipeline methodology.

Traditional Farming	Infinite Pipeline™
You only focus on top 20 percent of installed accounts, forsaking all others	You're able to touch all your accounts equally if you want to

Traditional Farming	Infinite Pipeline™
You're constantly calling customers and trying to sell a logical upgrade	You use all avenues to find out what is important to the customer for their next step or upgrade, or even a different product
You're always spamming, interrupting, offering unnecessary updates	You're updating via the community; asking customers what's interesting, relevant, or needed
Invisible references – you're not the first to buy but we can't tell you who else has	Open references, communities of practice, mine the data for problems
Customer product problems are not your job	You are listening and can help, or let customer service or the community help
All roles are separate and siloed; marketing, customer care, service, support, and legal don't communicate	All company stakeholders collaborate in an internal community to increase customer value
Company assumes customer will remain loyal no matter who the sales rep is	Customers are loyal to the community because the company hears them and constantly provides value
False interest in customer voice	Customer voice is heard as part of a chorus
False interest in customer satisfaction (one survey a year)	Continuous customer satisfaction and input
What the company says is law	Community tells you how it really is
Point in time account reviews; one and done; "I'll call you when I need more revenue"	Constant reviews = constant sales

Here's an example of bad farming. Mike held several licenses for large enterprise database software from BigDB. Periodically (and more often than he'd like), the sales rep called Mike to check in, offer "free" assessments or expensive training, and other things Mike didn't want. He knew that he'd hear from this lady toward the end of every quarter and often let her calls go right to voice mail. Mike calls this basic life support — keeping the relationship barely alive. It's not really anything more.

One day Mike got an obnoxious email from BigDB Global Finance (License, Support & Consulting) in Romania telling him that his support contracts on three of his licenses had lapsed and due to the lapse, the yearly maintenance cost per license was now tripled, in perpetuity. It turned out that BigDB had been sending invoices to the "ship to" address, the data center where the licenses were installed, and they'd been discarded.

Obviously several things went wrong here. The farming sales rep wasn't clued in to the impending problem and so couldn't have done anything about it. She was also useless in getting the problem resolved, even after involving her regional manager and BigDB's senior management. The licensing people were helpless to bend the process of penalizing Mike's organization for BigDB's mistake. Mike ended up buying three new licenses since it was cheaper in the long run than paying the penalty in perpetuity. So the sales lady got more business but, needless to say, Mike was no longer a referenceable client for BigDB.

Compare this story to the experience of one of Robbie's customers (whom Robbie had landed using social media). The customer signed a contract for a certain number of transactions per month for a software as a service (SaaS) supply chain product. During the install, Robbie's company had discovered and resolved a problem that had previously prevented some of the customer's trading partners from being visible. The first month, due to being able to see and interact with these additional trading partners, the customer's sales went through the roof, racking up 50 percent more transactions than they had signed up for.

Robbie called up the customer and gave him the news that he'd be owing Robbie's company a lot more than they thought (but, significantly, with no penalty for going over the contracted amount). His contact was delighted to pay more because they'd had a record month. Since Robbie's company allowed customers to contract on a month-to-month basis, the customer gladly signed up for an increased number of transactions per month.

By tying customer success with Robbie's company's success, what could have been a difficult conversation — your next bill is going to be 50 percent higher than you expected — turned into a reason for both parties to celebrate.

Where to Go Next

OK, we've been teasing you about the Infinite Pipeline all chapter long. The next chapter explains the basic concepts and a bit of the how-to.

If you think you've learned enough about Infinite Pipeline and you're raring to start planning your online presence, see the chapter *Your First 30 Days on Social Media* on page 109.

Infinite Pipeline™ Concepts Explained

*The salesperson of the next century will sell perspective and ideas,
not products or even solutions, so like every other transformation
that the American — and now global worker — has encountered,
the new era salesperson has to adapt, change and
find a new way to bring value.*

Ken Powell
*VP Worldwide Sales
Enablement, ADP*

Back on page 33 we showed a chart comparing the three evolutions of sales: Sales 1.0, born at the turn of the 20th Century, Sales 2.0, born way back in 2007, and Infinite Pipeline, born right now. We promised we'd get back to the qualities and concepts of Infinite Pipeline, and we consider each of these elements in turn in this chapter.

You'll notice that some of the characteristics of the Infinite Pipeline involve more than just the sales folks at your company. And that's good. Sales should be everyone's job.

It's All About Customer Satisfaction

You probably already know that satisfied customers buy more from you. That's truly a duh moment, right? But how much can you, the lowly sales person, actually influence customer satisfaction? As we've noted, you can avoid ticking them off by not constantly calling them. You can sell them what they need, not what you have to move today. But once the implementation is over, how much can you actually help them be satisfied? You're not even involved until you can sell them something else.

In Infinite Pipeline, you not only have major responsibility for customer satisfaction, you are part of a team — that internal community we've talked about — that can do something about it. And your customers are part of the Infinite Pipeline external community that helps solve their problems. Got an implementation problem? Post in the customer community. Chances are good that there's another customer who has a solution. Want new features? Product management is listening.

In his SellingPower blog,[30] Gerhard Gschwandtner details a variety of compelling statistics about the importance of customer satisfaction:

- A recent study by Accenture of more than 4,100 companies around the world found that 67 percent were moving their business as a result of having received poor service

- Another Accenture study of 16 retail banks found that converting customers from a low to medium level of loyalty and from a medium to high loyalty can yield a 20 percent increase in profitability per customer. For some banks in the survey, this translated to $6 billion in incremental profit.

- According to Bain & Company, an increase of customer loyalty by 1 percent represents a cost reduction of 10 percent

Infinite Pipeline is all about delighting the customer. By aligning the internal resources that can improve customer satisfaction and providing a customer community to help solve problems, your company can greatly improve the customer experience and customer satisfaction.

Because of findings like those we quoted above, many large companies are becoming part of a customer satisfaction movement, to the point that a new buzzword, Customer Experience Management (CEM or sometimes CXM), is becoming more popular. The goal of customer experience management is to move customers from satisfied to loyal and then from loyal to advocate (what we call an evangelist).[31]

Gschwandtner lists[32] the six key ingredients for CEM success:

- Map your customer touch points and appraise the quality of your customer conversations

- Shift from a company-centric to a customer-centric model

- Invest in the best software solution to manage CEM and create the right metrics

- Collaborate with the best thought leaders

30 Gerhard Gschwandtner's Do Your Customers Sabotage or Promote Your Success? Part I: bit.ly/LvP8iP
31 Customer experience on Wikipedia: bit.ly/JZGtLk
32 Gschwandtner's Do Your Customers Sabotage or Promote Your Success? Part II: bit.ly/MNSkfh

- Appoint a chief customer officer who reports to the CEO

- Reward your team for creating relationships that turn customers into promoters of your business

To implement Infinite Pipeline, you'll need to do these things, and more. Of course, as a sales person, you may not be the one to lead these changes, so perhaps you should recommend our companion book, *The Infinite Pipeline: How to Master Social Media for Business-to-Business Sales Success, Sales Executive Edition.* Of course, we'd be delighted to design an Infinite Pipeline program for your organization and train you how to implement it.

To implement Infinite Pipeline, you need to commit to improving customer satisfaction, as well as a number of other organizational and policy changes that we detail in the following sections.

Customers and Evangelists Provide Sales Leads

At the center of the Infinite Pipeline concept are two communities:

- An internal, sales-focused community incorporating your company's sales force as well as sales support, customer care, marketing, product engineering, product development, product management, communication, finance, advertising and PR, and your executives

- An external problem-solving-focused community comprising your current and future customers along with many of the internal sales-supporters who are also involved in the internal community

These two communities mesh to provide a virtuous circle in which a comprehensive internal understanding of customer need that:

Fosters the creation of new solutions that delight customers

Cultivates evangelists (AKA brand ambassadors) who spread your message far and wide.

As a sales person you may not be able to create the Infinite Pipeline community spaces we describe in the book, but you have all the tools and access to turn static clients into ecstatic clients. You also can help identify the ecstatic clients who can, with some support from you and your organization, be turned into active evangelists for your product or solution.

The first step is to change your thinking about your contacts.

Don't think of contacts as isolated CRM records or phone lists to which you have appended some personal details. Instead, think of them as a community, with you as the community manager. Constantly be thinking of how you can connect the people you know for mutual benefit. Good sales people already do this, helping customers or prospects find resources to solve problems their products can't solve. Use this simple technique to create a problem-solving community of your own, which will help you build your personal brand as the go-to person in your product category.

You can use this technique both outside your company and inside. For example, you may already feed back customer suggestions for new products or product changes to your product development folks. Make that a regular practice and you can help your company create those ecstatic customers.

We go into more detail about each of the Infinite Pipeline communities in the following sections, but both the internal and external communities have a number of characteristics in common:

- **One hand knows what the other is doing** — Just as all your internal partners are communicating on the same page, they are also communicating honestly and transparently with customers and prospects. When people in the external community feel that they know what you are doing, and how you are working to solve their needs, they will not only become more tightly bound to your brand, but also will begin to contribute ideas you can use to build better solutions.

- **All members help one another** — Internally, you've set up compensation so that all are incented to play an active role in creating new sales, whether it's through better marketing and lead generation or more customer-centric product design. The same thing happens externally, where customers help customers solve their problems, whether or not the solutions involve your products.

  Externally, you become a data miner, with a built-in, perpetual focus group to provide you with product suggestions and leads. You are simply paying attention, monitoring, and grabbing opportunities rather than constantly bugging customers to buy. By paying attention to trends, events, and business problems, and getting to know the clients from a business, personal, and importance standpoint you can more easily sell at the right time — when they're ready to buy.

These techniques fly in the face of traditional sales approaches because they require timing and reward waiting, something that sales people aren't too fond of. But if you've been selling for a while, you know you can't create customer needs out of thin air — just because it's the end of your quarter, it doesn't mean your prospect needs what you're selling. Instead of pushing end-of-quarter deals, you're waiting and learning more about your customers' needs.

If you're managing sales properly and selling at the right time, sales is no longer 50 percent luck. Instead of fishing, it's more like shooting fish in a barrel.

Solving Prospects' Problems

It seems obvious that you shouldn't just sell customers the stuff you need to sell, but rather sell them solutions that solve their problems. If you're not adding value, you're not asked back.

Remember the story we mentioned earlier in the book about the customer who asked not to be contacted again for 90 days, since they were going to be very busy implementing what they had purchased? When another sales rep called the company wanting to sell them the very same thing, naturally, the customer hit the roof.

This sort of behavior drives customers crazy. When you sell this way, you're trying to solve your problem — quota, end of quarter — not the customer's. So instead of being annoying, you should strive to be relevant and to add value. Try to be the resource that can connect customers with a solution, even in areas outside your product line or product category. Better yet, let your evangelists do this for you.

Compare the sales-oriented misfire experience with this problem-solving one. Robbie had networked with a leading consulting firm (we'll call them BigConsulting) on LinkedIn and developed them to the point where it was time to have a meeting to talk about selling Robbie's solutions into their customer base. BigConsulting showed up and wanted to talk about three of their clients, saying, "Two of these are definitely in your wheelhouse; the third we're not sure about." They were right. Two were right on. The third needed a solution Robbie's company didn't provide.

Rather than saying, sorry, we don't do that, Robbie's boss said, "I know the CEO of a company that does that. Let's call him right now." Robbie's boss texted the CEO, who said he was free. They called him from the conference room, confirmed that the other company provided the solution, and set up an appointment for BigConsulting to meet with the CEO.

Now you might think that this little turn of events was a surprise to the consultants, but it wasn't. Robbie had originally approached them about how he could help solve their client's problems and said if he could sell them something, that was great, but he would help BigConsulting find a solution no matter who provided it. At the end of the meeting, the BigConsulting consultants said, "We came here because we knew that even if it wasn't you guys, you'd know the right people." That was the approach and the relationship that Robbie had built, using Infinite Pipeline techniques.

As a result, the new relationship with BigConsulting brought several other deals to Robbie's company.

Answering Buyers' Questions

Most buyers know the basics of your solution before you talk with them, as we pointed out in the beginning of this book. Therefore, when you have a sales meeting, you're essentially there to answer the questions their research couldn't.

Rather than barreling right in to your presentation, trotting out your deck dreck with all your client's logos and your market share numbers, try starting the meeting by asking simply, "What do you know about us? What do you want to talk about?"

When BigConsulting brought Robbie a new prospect, one of Robbie's colleagues prepared a 40-slide deck. Robbie took a look at it and said, "There's no way we're presenting this. I'm giving them a call right now to confirm the meeting. Send it on over to them before I get on the phone with them." Confused, his colleague did so.

Robbie called the prospect and said, "We're sending over a big deck but there's no way we're going to present all this at the meeting. All we're going to present is six slides, but we put together a ton of others that might be relevant. They're for your reference, and to help you figure out the questions you'll want to ask at the meeting." The prospect said, "Thank God! When I saw that the presentation was 6 megs I almost died. The first six slides are perfect. I'm kind of glad you called me because if you hadn't, I might have canceled the meeting."

When they arrived at the meeting, Robbie said, "We're not really here to talk to you about my company. There are a couple of slides we'll go over, but after that, we'll open it up for conversation." The meeting ended up being 85 percent discussion and white boarding how the solution would fit and only a few minutes on the deck. The prospect actually appreciated the big deck, saying it would be great to show to their team members who had not taken part in the meeting. In fact, Robbie's contact called later and said a team member in marketing had a question on something in the deck. The contact said, "It was of interest to him, but not to me, so we hadn't really covered it in our meeting."

Focusing on prospects' questions and leaving behind more detail for them to refer to later puts the customer at the center of the engagement, where they belong.

Tailor your answers so they include your solution but deal with the business problem. This is different from solution selling; it's problem solving.

But above all, don't try to fake it. Mike approached a vendor of Web analysis software to find out more about their products. Yes, he'd done his homework, poring over their Website and reading blogs and comparisons, including the ubiquitous Gartner Quadrant and Forrester Wave. After making several attempts via their Website to get a sales person to call (really), he was referred to their "government solutions division." Cool, he thought, they know that governments, not being online merchants, have different needs. The meeting was set, and BigWeb started their presentation. Very soon into the meeting it became apparent to Mike that the sales person had just taken a standard BigWeb presentation, cut out a few slides and did a search and replace on a few relevant terms to make it government-friendly. Some of the bullet points didn't even make sense.

BigWeb instantly lost credibility by promising to speak Mike's language, but faking it.

Robbie's favorite approach to initial conversations with a prospect would have worked better. Robbie generally starts out saying, "I don't even know if this is going to be a fit for you." Not "This is the best thing on the market." Not "Guaranteed not to rust, bust, or collect dust." But a very simple statement that gets the prospect on your side.

Creating doubt that your product may not be a good fit not only lowers the temperature of the conversation, it makes the prospect try to sell themselves on the solution. You'll often find a prospect will engage more, and spend more time on the solution, if you involve them in this way.

Internal Sales-Oriented Community

As we said at the beginning of this chapter, the Infinite Pipeline involves an internal as well as an external community. You may not be able to get your organization to officially create either of these communities (despite giving your boss our *The Infinite Pipeline: How to Master Social Media for Business-to-Business Sales Success, Sales Executive Edition.*)

You can, however, go a long way toward fostering the team approach to selling improving communications with the team that helps you sell.

Sales 2.0 introduced the concept of getting sales more intimately involved with their natural enemy, marketing.[33] Infinite Pipeline takes this further, involving

---

33 Arturo Munoz' *Why Sales and Finance Hate Marketing* on YouTube: bit.ly/KSAOSd

more if not most of the other departments in your company in the sales nurturing process. Nobody gets paid until somebody sells, so sales is everybody's business.

Natural functions to include in this community start with sales force and sales support, and extend to customer care, marketing, product marketing, product engineering, product development, communication, finance, advertising and public relations, and company executives.

Ensuring that all these units know how they affect sales and what major sales efforts are ongoing is the main purpose of this internal community. This concept goes beyond Customer Relationship Management (CRM), with its emphasis on record-keeping that has become its Achilles heel. By providing a place for the company to manage the customer experience by collaborating, creating relationships, passing leads, and in general constantly trying to help sales, the Infinite Pipeline can establish a self-documenting, ongoing system for turning prospects into repeat customers and turning static customers into ecstatic evangelists.

Getting everyone committed to improving sales is perhaps this community's most important function. One way to do this is to change compensation patterns: Pay everyone for leads. Award badges for working to develop business. Incent employees to develop relationships with prospects and customers. Give bonuses for solving sales problems. Once again, this is probably a job for your management, but you can put the bug in their ears.

Many of the participants in the internal community will also engage with customers in the external community. You might think this is traditional customer service, but it's not. It's the tip of the Customer Experience Management wedge.

Social Customer Service

An integral part of the Infinite Pipeline, social customer service is more than just letting your customer service folks post on social media. To transform your existing inbound customer service center into a proactive social customer service team requires moving beyond telephones and scripts to social media listening and outreach.

Why should your company get involved in social media monitoring and response? Market Force Information, a customer intelligence firm, says these functions are becoming essential for enterprises, "Because the impact of negative customer experiences has never been greater for brands. With the ability to instantly broadcast their frustrations, consumers can turn a single adverse instance into a PR nightmare. Estimates show that defecting customers will typically share their negative experiences with eight to 10 people, and one in five will tell 20 people. Yet, a well-handled response can actually increase loyalty."[34]

Here's an example of the effect of one simple aspect of customer service: problem resolution timeframe. According to a study by the Corporate Executive Board,[35] failing to respond to a customer within a promised time period hurts their satisfaction far more than simply making a less-ambitious, and probably more-realistic promise.

Of course, you may think that, because you're B2B, this sort of thing doesn't apply to you. Baloney. Your customers typically know each other, and probably communicate on a regular basis. If they're not doing so on social media at the moment, they will be in the future. Take a look at a really basic, old-style, bedrock B2B industry like machine tools. Participants from all levels of machine tool companies are talking on a vibrant social community called CNCzone.com, which boasts close to 175,000 members and more than 850,000 posts. You think getting bad-mouthed on this site won't damage your sales prospects?

As we've said, B2B customers in every industry are increasingly turning to social media, looking up reviews, reading blogs, and sharing opinions on LinkedIn groups or Twitter. You need to not only be aware of what's going on out there, you need to be present, not only to counter the negatives, but to build good will. One step to doing this is to transform your current customer service function, which is probably primarily based on taking calls from customers with questions or complaints, into a social-media-enabled extension of your marketing, sales, and other Customer Experience Management efforts. And then integrate your Customer Experience Center into the Infinite Pipeline internal community.

Your Customer Experience Center is on the front lines of collecting information — social intelligence — about customers. While your company may assign the responsibility for gathering and interpreting social intelligence to a different department, your social customer service center can be instrumental in quickly spotting trends and summarizing what different customer segments are thinking. This social intelligence should be shared widely throughout the internal Infinite Pipeline community.

34 Market Force's *Market Force Sees Rising Demand for Integrated Social Media and Call Center Services*:
bit.ly/rFwUq4
35 Corporate Executive Board's *Stop Overpromising to Your Customers!* bit.ly/Pp2cwL

External Customer/Prospect/ Evangelist Community

The same people who are part of your internal Infinite Pipeline community are good candidates for the external community as well. In many ways the external community mirrors the internal, with one major exception: the external community includes customers and prospects.

Like the internal community, the external Infinite Pipeline community is dedicated to problem solving. Not sales. Seriously.

While your brand is likely to be all over the external community, if customers and prospects feel that the only reason to be there is to be sold to, they won't come, or if they do, they won't stay. Think about it. Would you hang out online with a bunch of sales people who are hell-bent on selling you something all the time? Of course not.

But, on the other hand, would you join a community that helps you solve your problems? And includes lots of your peers and industry leaders? One that enables you to increase your visibility by help solve others' problems? And which gives you access to product development people? Why wouldn't you join a community like that?

Is there product information available in the community? Of course. But there are also people who have implemented your solution successfully, who can offer tips and tricks. Can you set your next sales call in the community? Possibly, but it's far more likely you'll get ideas for your next product and create relationships that enable you to sell without pitching.

In fact getting information about customer needs that you can turn into products may be the most important function of the external Infinite Pipeline community. There are many companies already benefiting from this approach. For example, years ago, based on a suggestion in their external community, Dell created a Linux-based laptop product in two months that made more than $100 million and spawned a whole current line of similar products.

In the B2B space, SAP has pioneered using external communities to create and prototype new products with their Idea Place[36] and SAP Research Prototypes[37] communities since 2003. Notice how their framework integrates their third-party social presence with their community presence.[38]

---

36 SAP's Idea Place: **bit.ly/JqEFtv**
37 SAP Research Prototypes: **bit.ly/Jvu2lC**
38 SAP's Community *Roundtable Presentation: SAP Community Network Social Media* (PPT): **slidesha.re/LAjtDK**

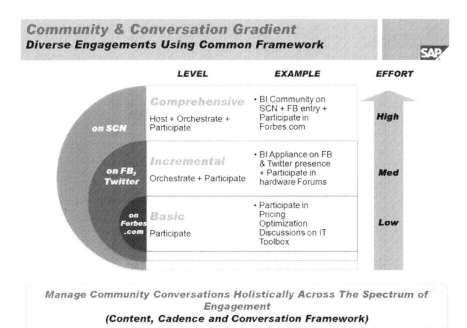

Figure 9 — SAP's Community and Conversation Framework

SAP's strategic goals include:

- **Build and Harness Communities** — of prospects, users, developers and partners
- **Amplify awareness and purchase consideration** — to bring SAP into purchase consideration set
- **Enhance demand generation** — by enhancing lead gen and nurturing programs
- **Accelerate adoption and end-user nurturing** — via richer and proactive engagement of end-users
- **Extend market coverage** — by enablement of developer & reseller partner community

As you can see, this is a mature strategy. SAP has laid out the following goals that support this strategy:

- **Awareness** — evangelize SCN
- **Immediacy** — real time

- **Reach** — broaden audience

- **Engagement** — connections

- **Reputation** — social media leader

- **Conversion** — to contributor, customer

You can tell these guys have been working on this stuff for more than nine years by the complexity of their vision. The communities have paid off, yielding:[39]

- 115,000 contributors in 2010

- 2,000+ Active Contributors in 2010

- 129 Topic Leaders

- 100 SAP Mentors

- 7,180 ideas contributed, with 183 turning into actions

The rest of the B2B industry trails in SAP's wake. Yet there is solid research showing that the time is ripe for social media engagement by companies. Jupiter Research found that while only 12 percent of companies provide customer-facing forums on their site, 41 percent of customers had consulted forums over the past 12 months regarding purchases they were making or intended to make.[40] Cisco Systems found back in 2003 that their customer community solved more than 150,000 customer issues per month that would otherwise have gone to phone-based (that is, expensive) support.[41]

If you do a lot of customizations for your product, you may be able to aggregate client requirements via your community and create a niche product instead. Sure, you'll accept a little less short-term profit from a custom project, but you gain a possible long tail of customer demand and will certainly improve customer satisfaction. In this example, product development gets a focus group, the customers in the community get a cheaper solution, plus you can ask customers to canvas their peers about the need, thus creating prospects for a new niche product and yielding built-in sales.

But of all the possible uses for your external community, identifying and developing evangelists (AKA brand ambassadors) can be the most powerful. We

39 SAP's *SCN overview Inside Track Sydney March 2012 (PPT)*: slidesha.re/NRTamv
40 Lithium white paper, *Online Community Best Practices: Getting Real Business Value from Social Customer Engagement*: bit.ly/LjR7uq
41 *E-Support: How Cisco Systems Saves Millions While Improving Customer Support* - Andrew Connan, Vincent Russell http://amzn.to/L0LUVz

talk a bit more about this idea in the section *Thou shall enable people to become online evangelists* on page 96, but for now, a simple definition of an evangelist will do: an ardent supporter of your product or service who gladly tells everyone who will listen about how great you are.

We prefer the term evangelist to the alternate brand ambassador term because, frankly, ambassadors are stuffy, bound by protocol, and not generally gonzo about anything. You want to find the people who are in love with your company and your products. You want to treat them well, and reward them for beating the bushes for customers. Often it's quite enough just to give them recognition, or perhaps small discounts. Sometimes just encouraging them is enough.

You have evangelists already, if your product doesn't stink. The trick is to find them, cultivate them, and enable them to spread the word and, of course, find more evangelists.

Using evangelists is really the only way you can scale the relationships you need if you're a company of any size, with thousands or hundreds of thousands of customers.

Now as a single sales person in your company, you're not likely to be able to accomplish all this. But you can start to think of your contacts as a community, and you can give them a place to go to discuss problems. A great way to do this, and to simultaneously enhance your personal brand, is to write a blog. Yes, we know. That's perhaps something you'd do only at gunpoint. But it's easy, and it's an easy way to start a community. We talk about how to start a blog in the section *Create a Blog* on page 173

What Not to do with Your Community

So we've told you some of the things you should do to set up your Infinite Pipeline external community. Now for a few don'ts.

Don't think it's all about the brand/product/service. In a working paper entitled *The Seven Deadly Sins of Brand Community "Management,"*[42] Susan Fournier and Lara Lee list seven misconceptions about customer communities, which they term brand communities. We provide our descriptions of each:

- **Brand community is not a marketing strategy** Don't let your marketing folks run the community! The community is a business strategy, not a branding strategy. Its focus is on improved customer experience. Problem-solving happens there, not message-pushing.

---

42 *The Seven Deadly Sins of Brand Community "Management"* : http://bit.ly/L0RpDG

- **Brand communities don't exist to serve the brand** Communities exist to serve the customers! We trust we've made that point sufficiently. Coke, one of the pre-eminent users of social media, is a company that really gets this. While we know they're not a traditional B2B brand (although one with huge institutional sales) check out this YouTube ad from Christmas 2011: **bit. ly/KqdLjn**. There's not a single mention of the brand in it. It's about family and people and feeling good. Coke understands that their main product, essentially sugar water, could be sold by anyone. Their difference is their connection with their customers. That's what you need to foster in your community. As Simon Sinek said, "People don't buy what you do; they buy why you do it."[43]

- **Build the brand, and the community will follow doesn't work** — Build it and they will come doesn't work. In fact, this myth is almost completely backwards. The reality is, build the community (and by build we don't mean just start one and hope) and it will build the brand.

- **Brand communities should not be love fests for faithful brand advocates** —If this is what you expect, then your community isn't going to go anyplace. The old saying of hold your friends close, and your enemies closer applies here. If your community doesn't feel like there's any place for dissent or complaining in your community, members aren't going to hang around.

That said, your Infinite Pipeline external community is a great place to identify, cultivate, and support your evangelists. Enable them to feel the love and they'll spread it around for you. The ideal situation is that community members feel they can say anything (within reason) and your supporters handle your defense without you having to lift a finger. Just don't expect the discussion to always be sunshine and moonbeams.

- **Don't just focus on opinion leaders to build a strong community** — Fournier and Lee put this really succinctly: "Opinion leaders and evangelists play important and well-documented roles in social networks. They spread brand information; they influence decisions; they help companies gain traction for new products at a fraction of traditional costs. But this does not mean that the most important community targets are the high-activity folks in the network." Indeed you need to make sure that all Infinite Pipeline community members feel they are supported and have a role in the community.

- **Online social networks aren't necessarily the best way to build community** Online is one way to build a community, but there are also plenty of real-

---

43 Simon Sinek's: *How great leaders inspire action*, Video on TED.com: bit.ly/NzpH7k

world ways, and nothing in this book should be read as encouraging you to focus only on the online. Obviously, if very few of your customers or prospects are online, you'll need to turn to other ways of creating community such as in-person events.

- **Successful brand communities are not tightly managed and controlled**
  If you think you should rigidly control your community, you're in for a bumpy ride. Communities belong to their members. You may be the sponsor, and an important voice, but you can't be in control. You can try, but you'll find that if community members don't have control, they won't stick around.

  Fournier and Lee put it this way, "Communities, by their very nature, defy managerial control. But letting go of control does not equate to abdicating responsibility. Effective stewards actively nurture, facilitate, and enable brand communities by creating the conditions in which they can thrive."

  We know of a large organization in which the director of communications had to approve every communication with the outside world. And we mean every letter, email, press release, and speech. Attempting to control risk by micromanaging the community won't work. If that's your organization, you'll need to change this tendency before you can create external communities.

We've probably already talked enough about how customers helping customers can benefit your sales effort. Your task is to enable the conversations that can make this happen. This means you're in the engagement business, and we're not talking weddings here. We're talking about keeping the conversation lively, and focused on serving participants' needs. We give you a step-by-step for accomplishing this in our *Infinite Pipeline Relationship Development Process* on page 167, so we'll leave it at that for now.

Salesperson's Contacts are Part of the Community

This may strike you as the most sacrilegious thing we've said yet. Of course, in Sales 2.0, you've been encouraged to turn over your Rolodex to the CRM system. If you're like many sales people, though, you still keep your best prospects to yourself.

Well it's a new age. Having the contact details for the big fish is not a big deal any more. Seriously, if all you're after is numbers to smile and dial, you've missed the point. Besides, your contacts are voluntarily putting themselves out there, and any sales person can get the digits, and a lot more, from sites like Zoominfo, which aggregates information about people from across the Web, and Jigsaw, now owned by Salesforce.com, where for every contact you share, you get access to a new contact. That's right. People are willingly giving up their 411 to gain access to a community of business cards.

So getting the coordinates of that prospect isn't the problem. As we said before, it's not who you know, but what you know about who you know. The most valuable information to a salesperson is not the number to dial. It's what you know about contacts in a community that helps you sell more. It's knowing who's ready to buy what you're selling. And the way you get that info is to get your network into the Infinite Pipeline internal and external communities, and share what you know about them, beyond title, budget, and buying timeframe.

Once in your community, these customers, prospects, college buddies, and your kids' friends' parents will let you know when they're ready to buy or when one of their connections need your products. All you need to do it is provide a reason for them to participate in community discussions.

Let's say you sell mid-market accounting software, for example. In your community, you'll want to have your existing customers — naturally — also any prospects you can coax — also naturally. However, you also want users of competitive products. Why? Because they are facing the same problems your customers and prospects are, and thus have a natural affinity. If you can get your customers talking about their problems and how they solved them with your software, the prospects and Brand X users will be interested. If any of these groups ask for help in solving problems, the community can become engaged in solving them.

And that's the goal: an engaged, problem-solving community that can help you determine who's ready to buy what you're selling. You can know when your customers are ready for your next upgrade, or next product, because you can hear them discussing their business problems. You can also determine the concerns of Brand X users by listening to them complain about their problems with their current software. You can get members to support your selling process because they are engaged and sharing their experiences with your products.

Notice the words we're using when talking about the Infinite Pipeline external community: hear, listen, engage. These are the key verbs — not advertise, push, dial, message, contact, sell.

Solve problems, and the world will beat a path to the door of your community.

Always Be Engaging Replaces Always Be Closing

In this new world of well-educated, crazy-busy B2B buyers, the venerable Always Be Closing (ABC) technique is more annoying than effective. In the Infinite Pipeline, ABC is replaced by Always Be Engaging (ABE). That doesn't mean you're not always alert for opportunities to close business. It does mean that you place more emphasis on the relationship portion of the relationship sell. And to do that means you need to develop a good sense of timing, which ABE can help you develop.

One of Robbie's contacts, let's call him Rick, moved into a CIO role at an account that belonged to a fellow sales rep. From the work that the rep had done in engaging the company, Robbie knew that Rick was in the middle of a big ERP installation, and was nowhere near being ready for their product. So Robbie called Rick just to find out how he liked his new job and, in the course of the conversation, asked how the implementation was going. Rick confided that there were some rough spots that they were struggling with on the ERP install. The CIO said, "We could really use some help with the rootey-rod installation that's coming up. My guys seem to be a bit lost on that one." Robbie told Rick that he could help out on that. "I'll talk to you in a couple of weeks to see if you're ready for our help with the installation. When you're ready, we can set up a conference call and maybe a meeting."

Robbie talked with the sales rep and they agreed that the rep would leave Rick alone until Robbie circled back with him. She said, "I take it we won't put anything in Salesforce about this, right?" "That's right," said Robbie. "I know there are other reps who are working on selling in the testing contracts and we don't need them hammering on my buddy at this point."

When Robbie called Rick back, he was ready to pay for Robbie's company's help, his colleague closed the sale on their add-on software, and later, when the CIO was ready, the testing guys sold in their piece.

Compare this approach with having several different reps blindly dialing the CIO and putting the hard sell on at the wrong point in the process. Robbie used the classic getting back in touch call not to hawk his wares — Always Be Closing — but to re-engage with his contact and to understand the challenges he was wrestling with — Always Be Engaging. He shielded his contact from having to fend off ill-timed pitches from other company reps and, using what he knew about who he knew, executed a coordinated, just-in-time sales plan that produced results.

Of course, you'll want to use ABE to engage with influencers as well as with prospects. Through research on social networks, you can identify internal sources of information and influence that you can cultivate. Recall how Robbie sold into the company whose purchasing guy had laughed at the thought that they'd ever buy from such a small company? The lady who was the key to that sale was not an executive, and not a decision-maker. Yet, she was able to push the right internal buttons to get the sale done.

Use ABE also to engage with folks selling products related to yours and share information on prospect needs. In fact, invite these reps and their customers into your Infinite Pipeline external community. This helps create a richer environment for problem solving — and sales.

Sales Reps are Immersed in Social Technology

Many recent online technology advances are no longer viewed as novelties and are now just business. For example, when was the last time you made a major purchase without first consulting customer reviews — a pioneering social media technique? When's the last time you thought twice about reading an online article or blog to stay up-to-date on your industry? Many other social advances are now considered table stakes in business: smart phones, mobile texting, and "checking in" to places.

You're soaking in social technology more now than ever before.[44]

Infinite Pipeline will be shaped by three technological forces that successful sales people will need to thoroughly understand. Gerhard Gschwandtner, in another great blog post,[45] calls them out, nicely summarizing many of the points we've been making in this book:

> First, mobile technology will deliver more relevant information to the salesperson in real time. As the windows of opportunity open and close faster, salespeople will have to recognize real opportunities faster and engage prospects with that relevant information.

> Second, the boundaries between buying and selling will become blurred through social media. Satisfied buyers will become the marketing extension of the seller. Buyers will collaborate with sellers around ideas that the sellers will implement and sell to the buyer. [There will be] an ecosystem where buyers and sellers sync their innovative capacities to actualize their "co-destinies."

> Third, sales technology will migrate from being sales-centric to being customer-centric. Imagine the impact on your sales if prospects were able to enter their data into your CRM tool and automatically create an opportunity whenever they have a need. Instead of advertisers attracting buyers, buyers would be instantly connecting to the best vendors, bypassing a Google search and connecting directly with the best and most competent salespeople. That would be the end of Google, and the company that created the technology would rule the world.

44 Palmolive's *"You're Soaking In It" (Commercial, 1981)*: bit.ly/L0tBiT
45 Gerhard Gschwandtner's *The Jaw-Dropping 3.0 Revolution*: bit.ly/Ke4yOv

There are a lot of points to ponder in these three paragraphs, but the overall message is that you need to master these new technologies to survive and prosper in the new sales realities.

If you haven't got one already, you need a smart phone. And you need to load it up with social media apps, including a way to access your Infinite Pipeline communities at any time.

You need to engage your evangelists through your community and on other social media. You need to nurture them, support them, and magnify their influence using what Gschwandtner calls an ecosystem, and which we refer to as the Infinite Pipeline communities.

Your technologies, and your approach, need to transform from being sales-centric to customer- and problem-solving-centric. Frankly this has always been true. There's an old adage that nobody likes to be sold, but everyone likes to buy. That's going to be truer than ever in the future. People will always be interested in buying solutions even if they lose interest in being sold them.

Measure Results

Using the Infinite Pipeline for B2B sales implies many changes for your organization. The change that has probably already occurred to you involves compensation.

When sales is a team sport, how do you compensate the players? Sales derived from Infinite Pipeline are likely to have many fathers and mothers, but your compensation plan is very likely concentrated on rewarding the sales person, and not the sales support staff, and almost certainly not the customer support staff.

Consider a sale in which a connection contributed by a line worker sparks a relationship developed by a customer service representative that is strengthened by endorsements from people whom your legal department and product marketing team suggest. The prospect joins the Infinite Pipeline external community where her assessment of your company is enhanced by the solutions your existing customers and your sales support staff contribute.

Clearly awarding a big commission to the sales person for the eventual sale doesn't adequately reward those who helped close the deal. And even a general company-wide quarterly bonus fails to recognize and encourage this type of teamwork.

We don't pretend to know how your management is going to solve this problem, but the good news is, through Infinite Pipeline, you can measure all of these customer touchpoints, which will provide a data-driven basis for unraveling the compensation problem. And, of course, we can help you figure it out via an engagement.

We hope you can see, however, that using these metrics is light years beyond compensating sales people for numbers of dials or other semi-objective measures that actually have little relationship to the sale.

You may already have a compensation model that is similar to what we're proposing. Many companies offer employees a spiff for referring a candidate who gets hired. The reason this tends to work well is because people don't want to be tied to a bad referral, so they bring good opportunities to the table. This principle also works with sales. Some team members may be tempted to take a volume approach, contributing a large number of leads of questionable quality. It would be easy to tie their performance to the quality of their leads, thus encouraging them to offer strategic, relevant leads.

Like we said, compensation patterns need to change with Infinite Pipeline, but the way each company evolves a new system will vary widely.

Social Media Sales Skill Sets

You may be wondering what kind of new skill sets you may need to prosper in the evolving sales environment. Well you can relax. You probably have most of what you need, but many sales habits and skills need to be slightly repositioned toward a much more collaborative approach.

In the table that follows we take a looks at the standard sales skill sets[46] both in the traditional setting and in the Infinite Pipeline.

Skill	Traditional Sales	Infinite Pipeline™
Closing The ability to ask for and obtain commitments	The end goal. It's over.	The beginning of the relationship
Differentiate The ability to stand out from the crowd	Feature, function, the competition sucks	Based on an understanding of trends, events and communities and your ability to solve problems and find fit

46 Skill set list and definitions borrowed from S. Anthony Iannarino's blog: **bit.ly/IRcYHb**

Skill	Traditional Sales	Infinite Pipeline™
Prospecting The ability to open relationships	Sales person should look for new business 60 percent of time (reality: <10 percent)	Community, customers, and prospects provide leads. Continuous planting and continuously harvesting — after a while you can't keep up.
Business Acumen A general understanding of business principles	Talk to prospects using company language. You understand your business; not necessarily their business or concerns. You have the hammer but don't know if they have nails.	Talk to the prospect in their language which you discover by researching in social media. For example: Carrie researched a CIO on LinkedIn and noticed he was very proud of his Project Management Office (PMO) accomplishments. She crafted an introductory note stressing her interest in PMO, and landed a meeting immediately.

Skill	Traditional Sales	Infinite Pipeline™
Diagnose The desire to understand	Trying to get prospect to recognize that they will die without your product; herd them toward your solution. Example: Dean called a retailer to try to sell them a payroll system. The prospect said, "Did you even look at the paper this morning? We just laid off 2,000 people. Do you think we need a new payroll system?"	Research prospect's industry, company and competition on social media to develop a general understanding of what is going on in their world so you can sound intelligent. Example: Robbie met with a prospect at a conference and said, "I see you're selling with Amazon." "We sell with Amazon? I didn't know that," the prospect replied. Robbie said, "Well, it's a good thing I'm here to tell you who your trading partners are. Now let's look at how I can help you communicate with them."
Storytelling The ability to share a vision	Usually it's, "Look at all our references!" Beat prospect to death with a huge volume of stories.	Finding a couple of relevant stories from your community and later showing them the volumes of references if they're interested. Robbie often says, "Here are two customers that are just like you. I have 300 more but these are the ones who are most relevant to your situation."

Skill	Traditional Sales	Infinite Pipeline™
Negotiation The ability to create win-win deals	Games, tactics, childish strategies – let incoming calls go to voicemail because I want them to think I don't need the business; don't seem overeager. Example: A CIO told us he had a sales person who called him over and over again about products that he didn't need. Finally the sales rep actually got mad at the CIO, leaving a message that said, "I can't believe you haven't called me back. Do you know how much time and effort I put into trying to reach you?" The CIO called the rep back, asked him to conference in his boss and read them both the riot act, asking them to never call him again.	You have already created the environment to win before you ever got into the deal.
Change Management The ability to help others improve	Not a strong point. Treated as an event. Drop off a manual and leave. Example: James' customer was a national restaurant chain. The CIO wanted to rip his company's multimillion dollar accounting system out, saying that nobody could figure it out. It turned out she was turning over her whole finance department every 9 to 18 months, so they were constantly training and never mastering.	You're constantly doing change management. Your internal community alerts you to issues before they become problems. You are constantly introducing new ideas, and laying the groundwork for new sales.

Skill	Traditional Sales	Infinite Pipeline™
Leadership The ability to generate results through others	Means managing up. Need to bring in the big guns to close because you lack authority. You're just one of the sprinkler heads.	You are running your own business. You are your own thought leader. Robbie once invited his CEO to meet with a partner because the CEO and the partner had a LinkedIn group in common. Naturally, his EVP of sales was a little nervous that the Big Guy was coming, but the CEO not only came, he stayed for the entire meeting and even presented.
Manage Outcomes The ability to achieve results	Metric-driven because of lack of trust. Final numbers are sometimes less important than the metrics, like dials. Need metrics to CYA in case the rep screws up.	You're always measured by results. You are measured by whether you make other players better, like Michael Jordan. Your leadership delegates to you, so you decide if you need the big guns to close the sale.

The New Sales Cycle

The Infinite Pipeline sales cycle differs from the traditional sales cycle as well as from the Sales 2.0 sales cycle.

The following table is based on a Sales 2.0 comparison from sales intelligence vendor InsideView.[47]

---

47 InsideView's *The Sales 2.0 Cycle*: **bit.ly/ICwPHl**

Traditional Sales Cycle	Sales 2.0 Cycle	Infinite Pipeline™ Sales Cycle
Discovery — leads from a built list are scored by marketing, then analyzed and qualified	**Search** — the new sales process begins with salespeople performing online searches for a target company from a built list	**Data Mining** — the sales process may begin from activities in the other two columns, but also begins through harvesting information from customers and prospects via social media and in the internal and external sales communities
Analyze — salespeople purchase business reports, search online company profile directories and use out-dated company Website	**Research** — salespeople find and understand the critical information related to the target company — company news, funding developments, new product releases, leadership changes, etc. — in a one-stop sales intelligence solution	**Leverage Relationships** —salespeople connect with prospects through social media as well as by asking customers, company employees, and other community participants for information and referrals
Definition — through cold call or elongated email setup, initial sales presentation is pitched detailing the benefits of the product or service	**Contact** — salespeople look up key company decision-makers and contact directly	**Introductions/ References** — the community makes it possible for salespeople to either get warm introductions or use existing customers as references

Traditional Sales Cycle	Sales 2.0 Cycle	Infinite Pipeline™ Sales Cycle
Initiation & Negotiation — introduction, discussion and finalization of sales terms for the product or service being offered	**Negotiation** — using traditional sales techniques leveraged with social media and sales intelligence insights, salespeople start the standard sales cycle	**Problem Definition & Solution** — by asking the prospect what they need and solving their business problems, the standard sales cycle is short-circuited
Delivery — product or service is delivered and followed-up with evaluation	**Close** — impressed by the knowledge and understanding of the sales angle and the benefit of the product/service, the customer makes the decision to purchase	**Continued Relationship** — after the first sale, the customer becomes part of the community, which helps identify and solve future problems/needs

The Power of the Network

All good sales people understand the power of a good network. You spend years building it up and you turn to it often for referrals, sales, and to track trends.

Social networking is actually not a strange concept to sales people. On the contrary, it's a way to maximize your current network by taking some of the friction out of the relationship process. Rather than trying unsuccessfully to get your contacts on the phone to talk business, you can engage them through social media on a broader level, often about topics that have nothing at all to do with business. Using social media to create more points of contact will help build trust, rapport, and familiarity.

Social media allows you to engage with the full person, not just the busy decision-maker who dreads getting one more touch-base phone call from you. That decision-maker has kids in soccer, enjoys flying RF model planes, is a Vikings fanatic, or has myriad other interests that he or she would love to talk about. As collaboration in organizations increases and as social media becomes more prevalent, finding champions in prospects' and customers' organizations is becoming more and more important.

You'd be crazy to call up a prospect and say, "Hey, I was just wondering how the big softball game went for your daughter's team." That would not only be creepy, your prospect would wonder why you're wasting their time.

But showing interest in a prospect's life on social media is not necessarily creepy at all. It's just what happens when you participate in social networks. Liking the prospect's post about her daughter's softball game is a low-risk way to show interest, and to be visible. Commenting on the post can also work depending on the stage the relationship is at.

So everything you know about relationship and network building is directly transferrable to use on social media. There are several new aspects you need to be aware of, however:

- **No stalking** — There's a fine line between being present in your prospects' social realm and being seen as a stalker. You'll need to feel out how comfortable they are in discussing non-business topics on social media with people in general and you in particular.

- **Don't be overly aggressive** — You'll also need to determine how up front you should be about deriving business from your social media network. We provide a step-by-step plan for beginning to engage with a prospect via LinkedIn later in this book. This proven process should be used for any initial social media contacts.

- **Be a Person** — You'll find it more effective if you share information about yourself on social media. Social media is all about relationships, and relationships can only be formed between people. Think about your offline networking. Probably your strongest supporters/referrers are people you know a lot about, and with whom you share non-business interests. You'll be more effective on social media if you enable people to connect with you on a wide variety of topics.

Common Connection Myths

There are a lot of myths flying around out there about how to use social media for B2B selling. We take on a number of them in the following table:

Myth	Reality
The minute I connect with someone I should try to get business out of them	Connect with people even when you don't need anything from them; people don't want to feel used; wait until the relationship has developed to the point where discussing your solution is appropriate
I have to connect with someone on LinkedIn for them to be valuable to me	You don't need to directly connect with a person for them to be valuable to you. Knowing someone your prospect respects and having them introduce you or recommend you is very powerful.
My connections are immediately going to overwhelm me with requests to be introduced to a contact of mine, so I need to make my connections private	Some will ask you, but you're not likely to be overwhelmed if you make your connections public. Ensure that anyone who requests an introduction can show value before passing them on.
Being there is good enough. You should be a LinkedIn Open Networker (LION) and strive to reach the maximum of 30,000 connections.	Really? If you were buying a car would you go to 30,000 car salesmen? To find a spouse, would you go on 30K first dates? Why does LinkedIn have a cap if having a huge, unwieldy network in which you don't know everyone is effective?

Large Community vs. Effective Community

It's common that people who are new to social networking think it's all a numbers game. It's not.

We know several people who, because they've reached LinkedIn's 30,000 connection limit, now spend hours removing useless contacts from their LinkedIn accounts so they can add new, slightly-less-useless contacts. If you're at the limit, what happens if you meet someone you really want to connect with? That's right; you need to remove someone else.

The reality is that you don't need lots of people you barely know in your network.

We belong to a network in which we can ask a favor from anyone in the civilized world. It's called the telephone network. Why doesn't it work to dial random phone numbers and ask for business? Because they don't know you, and you don't know if they have a need.

So you don't need a massive community full of people you don't know. You need to create a community that knows you, that will vouch for you, and that will connect you to new opportunities.

That community could be quite small as long as it contains quality contacts whom you can tap to answer questions and provide information that helps you land sales.

All networking boils down to a question of trust. People want to know and trust the people they're doing business with. We believe the fastest way to close a sale is to find a mutual connection to vouch for you. You've undoubtedly experienced this in your own career — the golf buddy or fellow soccer mom who happens to know someone who's buying.

What if you could connect with that one magic person whose endorsement would close each sale for you? That's your goal in Infinite Pipeline: develop connections with a community that can refer you and connect you.

Why a Large Network is Important

The preceding notwithstanding, there are some advantages to having a large-scale, well-connected network. In an effective Infinite Pipeline network:

- Most people are within a few degrees of each other

- People want to connect with other people, and can determine whether to trust you first

- Connection visibility shows how everyone is connected (see LinkedIn's three degrees of separation on page 94 for an example)

- It's not all about the product or service. The community provides value by providing expertise, problem-solving, and emphasizing person-to-person connections.

- When members change jobs and companies, you can keep them in the network and maintain your relationships because the network provides value

We can't pretend to know how large your network needs to be. But we're sure a smaller network in which the members have strong ties to one another will beat a 30,000 member LinkedIn connection pile any day.

Where to Go Next

The next chapter explains offers some cautionary tales about the downside of not managing social media properly. Following that are the 10 commandments of social computing. If you're anxious to get started learning more about social media, check out *Social Sites Defined* on page 94 and *Your First 30 Days on Social Media* on page 109.

Be Careful Out There!

We now have indisputable proof that online marketing,
YouTube and Twitter and all that it encompasses
is meaningful
and has arrived.
We are seeing real consequences to a mistake.
If [social networks] didn't matter, you wouldn't see this type of
reaction from J&J or consumers
[over the Motrin Mom faux pas].

Gene Grabowski, chair
crisis and litigation practice,
Levick Strategic Communications

Grabowski is referring to one of the entries in our Social Media Hall of Shame.[48] That entry reads as follows.

In fall of 2008, pain reliever brand Motrin posted a short video as part of an ad campaign aimed at young mothers. In an attempt to identify with its intended audience, the ad featured a young woman speaking in an irreverent tone about the "fashion" of wearing one's baby, and the back pain associated with the practice.

Some online moms found the tone patronizing and felt they were being mocked. The video went largely unnoticed for 45 days, but then on Saturday, November 15, one mother, Jessica Gottlieb, tweeted her disapproval using the Twitter hashtag[49] #motrinmoms.

By Sunday afternoon, #motrinmoms was one of the hottest hashtags on Twitter. Mommy Blogger Katja Presnal created a nine-minute YouTube video comprised of angry tweets from moms with baby carriers.[50] In all, however, fewer than 1,000 people posted using the hashtag. But this was a very vocal minority.

By social media standards, Motrin was slow to respond to the outcry. Yet by Sunday evening, they pulled the campaign, temporarily shuttered their Website, and apologized. Instead of engaging with the protestors on their own turf, however, Motrin reverted to an Old Media response: They tried to remove all traces of the video and ad campaign and offered a corporate apology in response:

---

48 Social Media Performance Group's Social Media Hall of Shame: bit.ly/HallOfShame
49 Hashtags are special Twitter keywords and are created by putting a pound sign (#) in front of a word.
50 The video *Motrin Ad Makes Moms Mad*: bit.ly/bZvjBR

"We have taken immediate action to respond to these concerns and have removed the advertisement from our Website."

By November 20th, they had pulled themselves together a bit more, and published a response with a much better tone. Kathy Widmer, Vice President of Marketing for McNeil Consumer Healthcare, offered a new apology that followed our mandate:**Be a Person**.

> So…it's been almost 4 days since I apologized here for our Motrin advertising. What an unbelievable 4 days it's been. Believe me when I say we've been taking our own headache medicine here lately! We are parents ourselves and we take feedback from moms very seriously.[51]

Much, much, **much** better!

Motrin's mistake was in not using the negative attention to engage in a dialog with the angered moms. By taking them seriously and listening to their concerns, Motrin could have probably defused the uproar and possibly turned the furor into an advantage. Engaging in a dialog would have enabled Motrin to explain that they were trying to be funny, and they were sorry that it hadn't worked.

Ironically, Jessica Gottlieb, author of the original tweet, said that she felt the ad did not need to be pulled. What if Motrin had originally addressed her directly and enlisted her help?

The Belvedere Vodka Fiasco

We'll tell one more tale of dumb company moves on social media: the strange case of Belvedere vodka.[52] This debacle happened on March 23, 2012 and involved a very short-lived and extremely offensive ad on Facebook (see next figure). The advertisement raised such a furor it was pulled within an hour, but that's not the end of the story. The company (or their advertising firm) posted a weak non-apology apology on Twitter and Facebook.

---

51 Read more about the Motrin debacle at bit.ly/awmztq
52 BuzzFeed's *Belvedere Vodka Pulls "Rapey" Facebook Ad*: **bit.ly/Losq09** and Time's *Belvedere Vodka Retracts Offensive Ad, Flubs Apology*: ti.me/KNqbFC

Figure 10 — Belvedere Vodka's Controversial Ad

Figure 11 — Belvedere's Non-Apology

Eventually Charles Gibb, president of Belvedere Vodka, apologized for real:[53]

I would like to personally apologize for the offensive post that recently appeared on our Facebook page. It should never have happened. I am currently investigating the matter to determine how this happened and to be sure it never does so again. The content is contrary to our values and we

---

53 Adweek's *Belvedere Vodka Apologizes for Rapey Ad on Facebook*: bit.ly/L1b4qv

deeply regret this lapse. As an expression of our regret over this matter we have made a donation to **RAINN** (America's largest anti-sexual violence organization).

This incident illustrates one of our central tenets — and the name of our book series — **Be a Person.**[54] Any company can make a mistake, and it's easy to offer "if anyone was offended" apologies. These won't wash on social media. People expect sincerity and transparency on social media. You should ensure that all your social media relationships, messages, and conversations engage your community on a personal level.

How to Use Social Media

We can learn two things from these object lessons:

Social media can bring a powerful company to its knees in the space of less than a week

With great power comes great responsibility[55]

We don't tell these tales to scare you, but rather to impress upon you the power and potential of this new communications — or, rather, relationship — medium. We also hope these stories, and the rest of the cautionary examples in our Social Media Hall of Shame,[56] demonstrate that using social media without a strategy and a plan may seem easy to do, but like juggling chainsaws, the outcome is much better when you're trained and prepared.

On the positive side of social media, take a look at the Blendtec YouTube videos,[57] one of the keystone case studies from our Enterprise Social Media Framework (ESMF).[58]

Blendtec makes powerful blenders, and so someone got the bright idea of doing a series of short videos called *Will it Blend?* Starting way back in 2006, and featuring Blendtec CEO Tom Dickson, each video — designated either "Try this at home" or "Don't try this at home" — blends a range of items from 50 marbles and a handful of golf balls to a new iPhone.

It was the iPhone blend video that went viral, racking up more than 9.8 million views, and counting. Combining the fetish power of the game-changing mobile phone with the eccentric idea of obliterating things with a blender equated to

54 Social Media Performance Group's **Be a Person** series: bit.ly/OrderBeAPerson
55 Spider-Man: bit.ly/InBePi
56 Social Media Performance Group's Social Media Hall of Shame: bit.ly/HallOfShame
57 Blendtec's YouTube channel: bit.ly/9pHXIh
58 Enterprise Social Media Framework: bit.ly/auxUYA

tremendous viralocity. Since the first iPhone bit it, the company has trashed a series of iconic electronic gadgets, including an Olympus digital camera, an iPad (11 million views), and an iPhone 4.

Was it planned this way? No. It was just a wacky — and cheap — bid for attention from a small company with a small marketing budget. It went viral because . . . well, just because it was bizarre, over the top, and cool, we guess. For almost no money, Blendtec has reaped more than 161 million YouTube views, 380,000 subscribers (making it #40 on YouTube's all-time list), and a 7X increase in sales.

So why do we mention this? Did you see the part about "almost no money?"

You could go viral as well, even in the B2B context. But to do so, you must be hooked into the zeitgeist[59] of your community, and the larger society. Offbeat, quirky ideas are what generally go viral. But if you try too hard (we're looking at you, LonelyGirl15[60]) you could do more damage than good.

Contrast BlendTec's success with the fact that the #1 result from a search on YouTube for Comcast is a video called *A Comcast Technician Sleeping on my Couch*.[61]

Talk about incredible results, both good and bad! Social media is here, it works for enterprises, it works for sales, and chances are good it is affecting your business today.

So What's Your Strategy?

From the preceding, it's easy to see that you don't want to go off half-cocked, jumping in on Facebook, Twitter, and LinkedIn without preparation and forethought.

Instead, like anything that's worth doing well, it's best to have a strategy for using social media. You may be tempted to listen to those in your business who have a "Hey kids! Let's put on a show!" kind of mentality regarding social media. It's so easy to get started, you may decide to listen to these folks and start creating a Facebook page, a Twitter account, or a YouTube channel right away.

We hope you will resist the temptation to jump in with both feet until you have understood why you are using social media, and how it is going to support your overall strategy.

59 Google zeitgeist: bit.ly/cy2fhg
60 LonelyGirl15's YouTube channel: bit.ly/dBib9J
61 A Comcast Technician Sleeping on my Couch: bit.ly/jPRrHZ

As a sales person, you probably are not responsible for your sales strategy. We recommend you work with your sales management (and get them to buy the companion book to this volume: *The Infinite Pipeline: How to Master Social Media for Business-to-Business Sales Success, Sales Executive Edition*) to create guidelines on how you will approach social selling.

External social media goals to consider include:

- Solve customers' problems

- Create strong relationships

- Thought leadership

- Community involvement

- Educate

- Inspire to action

- Share internal culture with external audience

Determine How Your Customers Will Benefit

If you can't quantify this, you need to rethink your whole strategy. If the answer is truly that you see no benefit for external stakeholders, that's OK. Just be sure you understand that social media only provides internal benefits for your business. As we've discussed, those benefits can be enough.

Plan to Evolve Your Strategy

Accept that you're going to make mistakes. You're going to learn what works and what doesn't, and so you need to figure out how you are going to incorporate continuous improvement into your social media strategy and practice. One important element of improvement is to be open to innovation from your staff. Chances are good many have significant experience in social media and can help suggest improvements.

Where to Go Next

The next chapter will take you through some guidelines for using social media to enhance your sales efforts. If you're anxious to get started learning more about social media, check out *Social Sites Defined* on page 99 and *Your First 30 Days on Social Media* on page 109.

The 10 Commandments of Social Computing

If you want to dominate the social media game, all of your effort has to come from the heart; and it can't come from the heart in the passionate, irrational, wholehearted way it needs to if you're trying to be anyone but yourself. Authenticity is what will make it possible for you to put in the kind of hustle necessary to crush it.

Gary Vaynerchuk, author
CRUSH IT! Why NOW Is the Time to Cash In On Your Passion

We've collected several rules for using social media as the 10 Commandments of Social Computing.[62] These rules are general and you might find it helpful to share them with others in your organization as you go about gaining support for the Infinite Pipeline communities or other techniques we propose in this book.

Thou shall not social network for the sake of social networking

Social Media is Not:	Social Media is:
A Fad	Relevant to the Enterprise
Just For Kids	For Everyone
About New Channels to Push Messages	About Creating Conversations
About the Tools	About Strategy
About the Techniques	About Planning and Execution

---

62 For other folks' 10 commandments, see:
bit.ly/c2L97N • bit.ly/9NWATb • bit.ly/c5s1ZT • bit.ly/ceUjEs • bit.ly/8ZNxQG

A Numbers Game	About Creating Relationships
A Replacement	A Supplement to Existing Techniques

Thou shall not abuse social networking

Quick Tips

- Don't push, push, push

- It's a conversation, not a soapbox!

- It's not all about you. It's about the relationships and community that you build.

- Avoid over-updating

  » Example: being 1 of 200 friends on Facebook, but making up 25 percent of updates — you're not that important!

  » Don't send out multiple requests to join your social media group or fan your page — If they want to join, THEY WILL!

- Avoid too many email blasts

Don't Push, Push, Push

People who do marketing are used to pushing their message out indiscriminately, hoping to somehow connect with those who will respond. In the traditional marketing environment, there is little way to identify ready recipients of the message, and marketers spend billions each year trying to segment the market and deliver the right message to the right person.

Social Media is different in three important ways:

- You can have conversations with prospects

- You can know more about your prospects and understand better how they will respond

- You can actually more-directly measure the effect of your efforts to attract and inform them

Because the medium offers these advantages, social computing users do not respond as well to the traditional push style of marketing. They may even be insulted if you blindly push your message at them.

Increasingly, online users respond better to relationship marketing.

It's a conversation, not a soapbox!

Avoid Over-Updating

If you're constantly updating your status, posting to your blog or otherwise creating a high volume of messages in your social media venues, fellow users are likely to see you as annoying.

For example, if you post a high volume of Facebook status updates, your friends may either tune you out or hide your updates. Or if you constantly invite them to farm with you in Farmville or take on the mob in Mafia Wars they may be tempted to unfriend you.

It's not all about you. It's about the relationships and community that you build.

Similarly, if your messaging is one-note — join my mailing list, buy my product, recommend my product — people will stop listening. You must balance your overt messaging with other messages of interest, either on or off topic. You'll need to discover the exact proportions that work for your community for yourself, but a good rule of thumb is to contribute four times for every time you ask for something.

Imagine you're at a cocktail party. You are making the rounds and you start to talk to someone who, although he's talking about a topic you're interested in, totally dominates the conversation and constantly asks you to come to his seminar and learn more.

Do you hang out with this person, or do you find an excuse to move on, and never re-engage with him?

Social media is like a big cocktail party. The boring monologists often end up speaking only to themselves.

How do you know if you're over-sharing? Ask. Often. But not too often!

Thou shall focus on connections and community

People join social networks to be a part of something bigger than themselves. So it follows that most of the time, that something bigger is not you (personally) or even your product or service. Remember, no matter how successful your presence is online, people will spend 99 percent of their online time elsewhere. So be careful to give them what they expect, and what they want, while they're at your place.

One of the main things people want online is for their voices to be heard, especially by others who are passionate about a product, issue, or topic. Enable that. Support their desire to be heard, to be valued, and to connect. What you say is important; what they say is essential. In other words, what you say is marketing; what they say is your brand.

Everyone is looking for a group that accepts them for who they are. Your job in creating a social media space is to foster that acceptance by giving them the tools, the space, and the permission to become a cohesive, self-sustaining — infinite — group. That's the Holy Grail.

People want relationships that translate into the real world, not just online! Nobody spends all their time online (well, they've at least got to answer the door and pay the pizza guy). Many people look to make their online time and relationships meaningful in IRL (In Real Life). There are many ways you can encourage these offline connections:

- Have real-world meetups[63] where virtual friends can press the flesh

- Show your followers evidence of how your customers love your products or services by providing testimonials — written and via video or audio — from satisfied and enthusiastic customers

- Encourage your followers to share details from their own lives, and how your business has helped them

Thou shall not commit social networking narcissism

Narcissus was so in love with his image that he gazed at it all day, to the exclusion of other activities. Sound like anyone you know online?

The Web is full of people who are full of themselves — the kind who might say, "Enough about me. What do you think about me?" Many enterprises act the same way online, showing an alarming sense of self-absorption. They may be talking with you, but conversation is one way — all about them, their business, their marketing program, their issues and obstacles, their successes.

---

63 Meetup.com allows people to organize real-world networking meetings online: bit.ly/btNB8n

One sign of social networking narcissism may be, as we've previously mentioned, constantly updating your status on Facebook, Twitter, LinkedIn, or other social sites. This is like push advertising and your contacts will soon tire of hearing all about you, especially if your status is boring trivia such as, "The line at Starbucks is long" or "My cat just rolled over" or "Going up the stairs." Yes, these are all real tweets!

Of course, you may be over-sharing about your enterprise as well. Remember, it's not all about you, your group, your business! You need to be interesting first, and interested always. This means you comment on other people's posts; you send them messages asking how they're doing; you help develop and sustain a relationship with your contacts.

Narcissism, self-promotion, and boring/excessive status updates are often cited as the top reasons people "unfriend" or disconnect with others online.[64]

Finally, the form of your communication also counts. Don't just make statements; ask questions, and especially open-ended questions, even if they're off-topic: What's your favorite movie? What's your best idea for promoting our products? What could we be doing better?

Thou shall balance business and pleasure in social networking

Social networking is supposed to be fun; don't make it all business. Don't be ultra-serious all the time. Sure, your business is serious, and important, but acknowledge that there are other sides to life, and don't be afraid to have fun. Make a stupid pun. Link to the latest stupid LOLCat picture (**bit.ly/dspJnq**) or dumb YouTube video (**bit.ly/9SQgex**). It's all about adding value, and sometimes that value is bringing a smile to your contacts' faces.

Remember, you are competing with all sorts of entertainment, online and offline. You may find that a light and humorous tone may attract more followers or deepen existing relationships.

Be a Person! Be personal. Share things about yourself. Ask others for their opinions. But be careful about offering your own, especially if they are controversial.

The more real you are, the better the online and offline relationship!

---

64 Reasons to unfriend: bit.ly/asCI5j

Thou shall be relevant

It's not about your agenda — Talk about what's important to your audience.

Sure you want to make your points about your products or services, but do so in relation to your audience's needs and interests.

One of the keys to social media success is providing what they want, not necessarily pushing what you want. Be relevant to their lives, even if it means straying off point. You want a relationship, a true, two-way understanding with your community. Think of the significant relationships in your life. How many of them are one-dimensional, built only upon a common interest in bowling, music, fishing, novels, disaster movies, or whatever?

Chances are in your best, most significant personal relationships, you connect on many levels. Ensure that you do that via social media as well.

Thou shall customize your strategy for your target groups

Before you even start using social media to improve your relationship with your community, be sure you know who they are, how they differ, and how they want to be addressed.

How can you find these things out? Ask them.

Take the example of Fiskars, the Finnish manufacturer you probably know, if you know of them at all, as a maker of scissors. Scissors. A pretty boring category. Who cares what brand of scissors you buy? How utterly, utterly dull.

Well, if that's the way you feel, you couldn't be more wrong.

Think about Fiskars' audience. What are they doing with the scissors (and punches, shape cutters, stampers, craft trimmers, embossers, knives and multitools, edgers, and other craft tools)?

They're scrapbooking and doing other crafts.

If you know any scrapbookers, you know they can be very passionate, even fanatical. And they are inherently social. They like to get together IRL (In Real Life) and swap ideas, and work on their projects together.

So Fiskars did a very smart thing, way back in 2006: They created the Fiskateers social media site.[65]

---

65 Fiskateers site: bit.ly/9oBR3R

How did they start their site? They found four women who were committed to scrapbooking and made them the heads of a nationwide campaign to create online and offline places (retail stores) for people bound by this common interest to gather and share ideas and community.

The site won awards. It generated results:

- 6,250 members in 50 states
- 1,000 certified volunteer demonstrators
- Craft stores where Fiskateers are involved Fiskars have three-times-higher sales growth than non-member stores
- 13 new product ideas/month
- 85 percent of "Fiskateers" are likely to recommend the product to a friend[66]

And, by the way, Fiskars spent less than $500,000 on this effort.

So you need to understand the segments of your target market. And you need a strategy for dealing with each. For sure there are some you will not be able to reach online. But a surprising number will not only respond to you online, they're already there and talking about you and your enterprise. Find their communities, listen, and tailor your approach to their needs.

So your question is: Can you find four women? (Or eight men.)

Thou shall balance online activities with real world activities

For best results, social networking relationships should translate into real world action of some kind. This action may be face-to-face (F2F) meetings, commitments to act to publicize or endorse your products, or some other action such as sales.

Social networking is a way to stay connected in between real world events. If your enterprise has periodic events, social networking can keep participants connected and top-of-mind in the intervals between real-world community meetings.

Social networking is a dynamic way to quickly get the word out about real-world events. Combine it with your normal online promotions, such as email lists, newsletters and online advertising.

If you put all your eggs in the social networking basket, you may one day realize that you've lost some of the real-world connections you built up over the years.

---

66 Adam Singer, blogging about Jackie Huba's (Church Of The Customer) Keynote at MIMA Summit Oct 5th, 2009: bit.ly/cPol5P

Thou shall not try to control everything

As we've discussed, social media is about the community, not about you. And that implies that you have to give up some control in order to do social media. You may be used to thinking you're in control of your brand, your message. Well, you never really were. What people think about you has always been your brand.

Leroy Stick, the anonymous person behind the satirical, faux BP Twitter account, @BPGlobalPR, perhaps said it best: "So what is the point of all this? The point is, FORGET YOUR BRAND. You don't own it because it is literally nothing. You can spend all sorts of time and money trying to manufacture public opinion, but ultimately, that's up to the public, now isn't it?"[67]

People have always talked about you (if you're lucky), and sometimes they say bad things about you. Now their talk is visible on the social Web, and you can see, perhaps too vividly, what your brand is, and what messages your community produces about — you!

To engage the community, you're going to need to give up control.

You won't control the conversation. You won't control the venue (close your site and they'll go elsewhere and bad-mouth you). You won't control how people react to you.

Giving up control is the toughest thing for all businesses — you're not alone!

Social networking is dynamic; it belongs to the participants; it's not about control, it's about empowering people and energizing them to act on your behalf.

Social networking is about relationships, and relationships are based on a level of trust, not control.

But what if people are saying bad things about me, you ask?

Face it, if you act in the world, you'll always have detractors. The difference social media brings is that now you can not only see what people are saying about you, you can react, in real time, and, by engaging them, perhaps change their minds.

This capability alone is worth giving up some control, isn't it?

Thou shall enable people to become online evangelists

Not only can you find the naysayers online, you can also find your supporters.

---

67 Leroy Stick's blog post on StreetGiant: bit.ly/btswHj

Your goal should be to identify, cultivate, and empower these supporters to become your evangelists.

That requires training, teaching them how to use tools, and how to bring the message to others.

The goal of social networking is not to be a one-person show, but to create an army of people to take the message out.

According to Jeremiah Owyang, formerly of Forrester Research,[68] "An evangelist's role is to go beyond understanding and get others to believe in your product or service. This is beyond just communication and advertising and gets to the fundamental root of human communications, building trust."

People are many times more likely to take a friend's recommendation than a stranger's. Building an army of trusted friends will multiple your current efforts many fold.

Where to Go Next

The next chapter presents explanations of various popular social media sites. If you're anxious to get started using social media, see the chapter *Your First 30 Days on Social Media* on page 109.

---

68 Quoted by Ashley Lomas: bit.ly/8YRqmf

Social Sites Defined

Social media are online communications in which individuals
shift fluidly and flexibly between the role of audience and author.
To do this, they use social software that enables anyone without
knowledge of coding, to post, comment on, share or mash up
content and to form communities around shared interests.

Joseph Thornley, CEO of Thornley Fallis

Social networking sites will come and go, but the approaches to going social that we describe in this book can be adapted for any site. With that said, let's take a look at some of the most popular and useful social sites and concepts out there, and give some quick definitions.

Facebook

Facebook is the largest social networking site by far, with a billion users. Many of its users use the site to keep up to date with friends and to "subscribe to" celebrities, popular TV shows and movies, and causes. However, many use Facebook for serious purposes such as recruiting talent, selling products, and creating communities around brands or products.

The major features of Facebook include friending — connecting with other users so that you can see their activities; posting statuses — short blurbs about what you are doing or interested in; reading what others are posting in your News Feed, a constantly updating timeline of the comments and activities of your friends; and playing online games such as Mafia Wars and Farmville.

LinkedIn

LinkedIn is the most professional of the popular social networks. Users tend to be more affluent and influential, and more of their interactions involve some business purpose rather than being purely social. LinkedIn is a great place to prospect for sales leads, find talent, or find partners and customers. LinkedIn is organized around your user profile, which is like a resume on steroids. In addition, users' profile pages feature a News Feed similar to Facebook's as well as any number of plug-in applications such as Reading List by Amazon, SlideShare, blogs, and others.

LinkedIn has many features that enable you to find and connect with other users, but you are limited in the number of people you can contact directly and/or connect with. LinkedIn uses a principle of three degrees of separation: those you are connected to are your first degree network; those whom your connections are connected to are your second degree network; those who are connected to your second degree network form your third degree network. You can only directly contact your first degree network, but can ask those contacts for help in connecting to people in your second or third degree network.

We explain this concept in more detail later in this book.

One of the most useful aspects of LinkedIn is their Groups function. Anyone can create a group and invite like-minded people to join. It's a great way to meet others who share your interests. Another useful function is LinkedIn Answers, which enable users to ask and answer questions on any subject.

Twitter

Twitter is what is known as a microblogging social network. Members post messages (known as tweets) of up to 140 characters and those who follow them see the messages in their News Feeds. Often derided as shallow, trivial, and boring, Twitter is used for sales, talent acquisition and all sorts of business and professional functions, including organizing online and offline events, and spreading the word about products and brands.

People who follow your tweets are called followers, and if they like a tweet they may retweet it — repeat it — to their followers. You can find people to follow by using the Twitter Website's search function to search for words or phrases, or for special keywords called hashtags. Hashtags are created by putting a pound sign (#) in front of a word, for example #socialbiz. People do this so their tweets can be associated with others on a similar topic. For example, many recruiters post their job openings on Twitter using the hashtags #job or #jobs.

Twitter is often used to call attention to a Website or a blog or other online destination. With only 140 characters to play with, it's hard to say anything complicated, and thus Twitter often serves as an advertisement for lengthier treatments of a subject.

Twitter Directories — WeFollow, Twellow, etc.

Twitter has spawned its own universe of related sites, including many different sites dedicated to helping users find tweets and tweeps (people on Twitter) of interest. Directories like WeFollow and Twellow enable users to list themselves, add tags describing their interests, and use tags to search for tweeps that share their interests.

Tweetups

A tweetup is not a site, but rather an offline gathering organized via Twitter. Organizations as diverse as NASCAR,[69] NASA,[70] and non-profits such as GiveMN[71] and Maui Food Bank[72] have used tweetups. Tweetups offer a chance for people who may only know one another virtually to meet in person. It's a great idea for enterprises because it can solidify interest and support for your products.

YouTube

YouTube is a free service that lets people post short videos. Users can create a channel to house multiple videos, and other users can subscribe to the channel, tag videos within it, and comment on them in text or by posting a video reply. In most cases, users can embed (insert) videos on their Websites without the poster's permission, thus providing a free source of content for their own Websites.

YouTube is the largest video service of its kind, but there are lots of others, such as Vimeo and Vevo. YouTube tends to be in the forefront of the social networking aspect of video. The site has rapidly gained popularity and is now the world's second biggest search engine as the growth of video content has outpaced the growth of text.

Since YouTube is the second largest search engine, using YouTube can help drive traffic to your business, other social media sites, and Website.

StumbleUpon, Delicious, Digg, Flickr

These sites are known as social bookmarking sites. Each provides ways for people to discover Websites, videos, blogs and pictures of interest based on the efforts of other users, who tag sites or articles of interest with keywords that others can find via searches. StumbleUpon will email you with suggested sites in categories that you select. Delicious and Digg enable you to search for keywords and will suggest general interest items. And Flickr specializes in photos, enabling you to post and tag photos and share them with friends.

According to Edelman's Trust Barometer,[73] people want news and product reviews from other consumers rather than advertisers or CEOs. The emergence of these types of social networks has reflected the participatory movement social media had created.

---

69 NASCAR Tweetups: exm.nr/fH5zR4
70 NASA Tweetups: bit.ly/hp0LXm
71 GiveMN Tweetup: bit.ly/dLTwXt
72 Maui Food Bank Tweetup: bit.ly/ggP0Tt
73 2012 Edelman Trust Barometer: bit.ly/NRnnnj

Blogs

Short for Weblog, blogs are a way to post longer-form articles that may include pictures and videos. The average blog post is not terribly long — perhaps 400 to 700 words — that usually treats a single subject. Some blogs are user's everyday thoughts, like a diary, and others examine technical, philosophical, or religious topics. The most popular blog site is the Huffington Post (now part of AOL), which examines political topics, but there are also popular blogs that follow celebrities (TMZ, Perez Hilton), technical gadgets (engadget, Gizmodo, TechCrunch), post satirical takes on current events (Gawker, The Onion), and many explore business topics (Seth Godin, The Economist, Tom Peters). You may be surprised to learn that the third most popular blog site is **BusinessInsider**, with more than 12 million visitors per month.

Anyone can create a blog, and tens of millions have. Wordpress, the most popular blogging platform, hosting more than 24 million blogs, reported that in 2011 more than 50,000 new blogs were created daily.[74] A significant percentage of those are started by people who are looking to make money from their blog. A blog is a particularly good way for enterprises to engage with their communities.

Google Alerts, Blog Search, Reader

Google has a wealth of tools to aid you in monitoring what people are saying about your organization on social media sites.

Google Alerts are automated searches you can set up that will search for keywords and email you the results regularly. At the very least, your organization should have some Google Alerts set up.

Google Blog Search does, guess what? Blog searches. It's another great way to keep tabs on the conversation.

Google Reader enables you to subscribe to RSS feeds (see below). Most blogs have feeds that Google Reader can consolidate into one place for you to read, sample, or skim.

Google+

At press time, Google+ was a young network with features similar to Facebook but with a more-effective way to organize your friends into "circles." The network exhibited phenomenal growth, attracting more than 10 million mostly male users in its first two weeks of operation. While many of its features are derivative, Google+'s Hangouts feature, which enables users to create ad hoc meeting spaces

---

74 Technorati's *WordPress.com Introduces WordAds*: bit.ly/PxkB86

that include video conferencing, may force other social networks to create their own equivalents. And sure enough, shortly after Google+'s launch, Facebook partnered with Skype and subsequently launched Facebook Video Calling in early 2012.

Google+ has a real potential to challenge Facebook for social networking dominance, although it has yet to show the kind of site engagement numbers that Facebook has. A related effort, Google's 1+ equivalent to the Facebook Like button, released in March, 2011, achieved broad acceptance in a phenomenally short period of time, and has been especially spurred by the release of Google+. By May, 2012, 13.3 percent of the top 10,000 sites had added a +1 button to their homepages, up from 4 percent in 2011.[75]

Google combination of a social network with its search engine dominance may eventually help it eat into Facebook's impressive social media dominance.

RSS Feeds

Standing for Really Simple Syndication, RSS is a way for users to "subscribe" to the updates of a site or a blog. Subscribing means that whenever the content changes on the subscribed-to site, an update is made available. You can keep up with the update by subscribing to the RSS feed using an RSS feed reader, like the free Google Reader. That way you don't have to constantly revisit the site to see if anything has changed. You should consider implementing an RSS feed for your own site and social media properties.

Social Aggregators — FriendFeed, etc.

FriendFeed enables social media friends to follow one another's' feeds from more than 50 social networks in one place. FriendFeed pulls friend activity from other sites and assembles it into a News Feed on its site. Users can thus just check the FriendFeed without having to visit several social sites to keep up with their friends.

There are many other similar aggregators, including Spokeo and new-kid-on-the-block RebelMouse.

Personal Curation

One of the fastest growing trends in social media, curation means helping others make sense of the daily fire-hose flow of information, links, pictures, and videos. Curation sites allow users to create and curate their own publications based on their social media activity and feeds.

The resulting magazine-like electronic publications feature articles harvested from, for example, the activity of a user's Twitter followers and Facebook friends. One of

---

75 Mediabistro's *40% Of The World's Biggest Websites Link To Twitter On Their Homepage*: bit.ly/MaTqO1

our favorites, Paper.li, scans and categorizes your feeds daily and creates short summaries with links to articles, blogs, pictures, and videos. The publication has a front page and multiple "departments" containing material in categories such as technology, business, and politics. See an example at bit.ly/MEDaily.

Summify is much simpler, presenting your top five news stories from your social networks, and delivering it by email, Web or iPhone.

Storify is less-automated, and enables you to curate your own publication by selecting specific material from Twitter, Facebook, Delicious, YouTube, Google searches, RSS feeds, and other Storify publications via a simple drag-and-drop interface. Whenever we encounter a lot of articles around a single subject, we'll go to Storify to create a rollup, known there as a story.

Scoop.it enables you to hand-curate a magazine based on a particular topic that includes only the articles you select. For example, our topic is Enterprise Social Media, and you can read it here: bit.ly/EnterpriseSM

Because it is hand-curated, Scoop.it takes more time. The service suggests various articles based on your Twitter and Facebook feeds as well as blogs and other social properties. You can add a bookmarklet to your browser and add any URL you happen to be viewing to your paper.

Scoop.it enables you to not only add an article, but to comment on it, automatically tweet it, post it to your Facebook wall, and add it to your blog.

One of the benefits of using curation tools, especially those that can automatically announce a daily edition, can be increased followers. For example, when our Paper.li publication comes out, the site automatically announces it via Twitter and Facebook and lists the Twitter handles of several contributors. These people are often pleased to be mentioned and may follow us back, retweet, or otherwise mention our publication. We've established several solid relationships with people based on this feature.

As the torrent of social information grows, more tools to enable users to filter and curate information will crop up.

Location-Based Sites — FourSquare and Facebook Places

With the rise of the smart phone, location-based sites have gone wild. FourSquare and Facebook Places allow users to "check in" either manually or automatically at real-world locations such as bars, restaurants, and other venues. The idea is to help provide a real-world connection for social-world friends. But detractors say the information these sites provide about where people are right this moment is an invitation to burglary or worse.

You'll want to consider whether to make location-based sites part of your social media strategy.

Expert Sites — Squidoo, About.com, eHow

There are lots of expert sites on the Web. Some are heavily curated (About.com has editors assigned to most of their expert areas); some are automated (Squidoo aggregates lots of content on a single topic); others are organized around how-to areas (eHow has articles and videos that show you how to do almost anything).

You should review these sites to see if they're talking about you and your company, and to determine if they might include your organization in their materials.

White Label Sites — Ning

White label social media sites provide the tools for you to build a standalone social media site for your organization. One of the oldest and best is Ning ("peace" in Chinese), which hosts more than four million sites. Incidentally, cofounder and Ning chairman Marc Andreessen created the first insanely popular Web browser, Netscape, back in 1996 and sold it to AOL for $4.2 billion in 1999.

Your organization can get started on Ning for a few dollars a month. Of course, first you need to know whether your community needs (another) place to go, and whether you're ready to commit to the effort necessary to create and host a community. Ning might be a quick way to test the waters for your external, or even internal, Infinite Pipeline communities.

Orkut and Bebo

Social media is a worldwide phenomenon, and while a large percentage of Facebook's membership lives outside the US, there are also social networks like Orkut and Bebo that focus on non-US members.

Orkut, owned by Google, is currently the ninth most popular social network with more than 100 million users. After starting as an invitation-only network in the US, its largest proportion of users now come from Brazil, where it is one of the most popular Websites, and from India.

Acquired by AOL in 2008 and then sold to hedge fund operators Criterion Capital Partners in mid-2010, Bebo was also started in the US and now has more than 40 million users, a quarter of which are from the UK.

If your organization wants to reach outside the borders of the US, consider using social networks such as these.

Knowem

Knowem is one of many sites that will allow you to reserve your organization's presence on hundreds or even thousands of social media sites. You can use the site to do this even if you have no plans to create a presence on hundreds of sites. It's a good idea because a) you may someday want to join one of the obscure sites and b) you may want to prevent others from usurping your identity on social sites.

Knowem is also a good way to research specialty social media sites where your community may have an active presence.

Influence Tracking Sites

Of course, it was inevitable that sites that measure and rank social media users' influence would crop up. The most famous is probably Klout, which ranks more than 100 million social media users and 2.7 billion pieces of content daily. There are those who find Klout's methodology — counting connections, number of social media networks, and other quantitative data – does little to measure true social media influence.

Since social media is not really a numbers game, but rather a depth of connection game, Klout comes up short in measuring the quality of one's connections and conversations.

Another tracking site, Empire Avenue, combines a social network and a public, stock-market-like marketplace to give a more-nuanced measurement of user influent.

On Empire Avenue, players buy and sell stock in one another. The site gives raw Klout-like scores for numbers of connections on various social networks, and users can interact with one another via shout-outs and discussion groups.

Players earn currency called Eaves and can use it to broadcast ads, send other users on missions (such as "Go Like this page on Facebook and get 500 Eaves") and buy luxury items that give various capabilities. The site awards badges (see below for a definition) for various achievements.

It remains to be seen how accurate this type of measurement is, especially since actively engaging on the Empire Avenue site is a large component of one's stock price. However, participation can yield a higher social media profile. Since beginning our participation in September, 2011, within a month we tripled the number of Likes on our Facebook page (https://www.facebook.com/SocialMediaPerformance) and got a hundred or more new Twitter followers.

Image Sites —Pinterest and Instagram

The latest darlings of social media at this writing are the image sites Pinterest — a virtual bulletin board for images taken from other sites — and Instagram, a mobile phone picture uploading site which Facebook purchased for $1B — amazing considering the site had nine employees at the time.

Marketers are interested in Pinterest, we think, because it finally looks like something they can relate to: advertising. The very idea of people willingly posting images of their products has got them hot and bothered. While it certainly makes it easier to identify users who like a particular product, Pinterest offers only rudimentary ways for marketers to interact with its users. But that's not a problem for advertisers who are used to blasting one-way messages out indiscriminately.

Attitude aside, Pinterest may yet turn out to be a great idea for sales folks. It's just too early to tell.

Instagram's claim to fame, on the other hand, is that it:

- Makes it easy to upload mobile phone photos

- Offers "filters" that alter the appearance of the photos to make them look old-timey or surreal

Of course, any hot mobile app these days is considered a great way to, wait for it, advertise to a new market. Recognizing this, in April, 2012, Facebook bought the site for $1B.[76]

Social Media Badges

Many sites provide badges, little graphics that represent the site or some achievement, to supporters who then post them on their blogs or other sites. One example of this is on LinkedIn. When you join a LinkedIn group, you have the option to display the group's badge on your profile so others see you're a member.

Badges are also given by sites like FourSquare to signify some achievement or status. It's a good way to enable and encourage evangelists.

---

76 NY Times' *Facebook Buys Instagram for $1 Billion*: nyti.ms/NUtiYz

There are also other types of badges that recognize achievements of your supporters, such as "Top Blogger" or "Most Valuable Evangelist."

Badges are a part of a trend called gamification. The term refers to taking some of the trappings of electronic games and applying them to other endeavors to help motivate users — players — to achieve their goals.

Where to Go Next

The next three chapters are all about getting started on social media. We advocate taking it slow if you've never done social media before, and we offer activities to do during your first 30, 60, and 90 days on social media.

Your First 30 Days on Social Media

Networking is not about hunting. It is about farming.
It's about cultivating relationships.
Don't engage in "premature solicitation".
You'll be a better networker if you remember that.

Dr. Ivan Misner
author & founder of
Business Network International

Here's the short list of what you'll need to do in your first month on social media:

- Decide on professional vs. personal use of social media

- Evaluate social media sites

- Create your messaging

- Sign up for LinkedIn

- Make sure your profile is as complete as possible

- Join 10 -15 groups – if done correctly you can add a million people to your network

  » 5 large networking groups (the executive suite)

  » 5 general groups around your field

  » 5 specific groups for your field

- Connect with family and friends, especially higher up business contacts (parents, golfing buddies, fellow club members)

- We go into greater depth on each of these points in the sections that follow.

Personal vs. Professional

We have to assume you're going to use social media professionally if you're going to try to implement the tips in the book. But what does that mean? It means that everything you do online must be professional and reflect well on your company.

Think Before You Post

We suggest you create a poster of the slogan below and distribute it to everyone in your organization.

Think
Before
You
Post

Many people have alienated others online through ill-considered statements and toxic encounters (see the previous chapter, *Be Careful* Out There! for a refresher). To avoid making a mistake, never say anything online you wouldn't want

- Your own family to see

- To see on a billboard

- To be published on the front page of the Wall Street Journal

You also need to consider the heft your enterprise may have. What you say matters when you are a "someone." Your enterprise stands for something. Thus, people are likely to listen closely to what you say. Think before you tweet/post — and think this: "If someone said this about me, would their organization or good name be harmed?"

Another thing to remember: Inauthenticity is the enemy of your social media effort. This means you need to truly understand the difference between using social media as just another one-way communication channel, and truly engaging your community.

One of the main techniques your community will hate is known as sock-puppetry: the disingenuous use of a real or fake user to parrot the enterprise's party line — just like sticking your hand in a sock puppet and expecting to be immune to criticism.

We collect a rogue's gallery of bad social media moves in our Social Media Hall of Shame at **bit.ly/HallOfShame**. It's a good primer on what not to do with social media.

Choose Your Targets

What kind of followers do you really want?

Chances are you don't want just any random people to follow you on social media. Think about your target audience. When you do, be sure you're not overly restrictive — only B2B buyers at director level or above, for example. Remember that there are influencers all over your prospects' organizations. What do they look like? What are they interested in? How can you win them over?

Don't necessarily accept all connections. It will be tempting early on. One of our customers, let's call him Ara, asked us to not allow any Twitter followers from outside the two states he does business in. He was angry that the previous managers of his Twitter account had pursued followers not only outside those states, but outside the country. When we began helping Ara, we convinced him to broaden his horizons. The next thing we know, he was direct messaging a follower from England who had a subsidiary in the States. As famous social media celebrity Guy Kawasaki said, "You don't know who the best evangelist will be for your product or service."

Just like you need to find a balance for how much you communicate on social media, you may also need to find a balance for the quality and quantity of communication by those you follow. Some people post about every little thing. Others rarely talk about business. Many may post dozens of times a day, making it hard to follow them. These people may not seem to be worth following at first blush. However, you need to keep in mind that your objective is a relationship, and sometimes business can come to you from someone you relate to based on music, or wine, or baseball.

Mike once reconnected with an old business connection just because they both liked the Doobie Brothers. Mike was using Pandora, the online radio app, and what he listened to was posted to Facebook automatically. Glen saw that post and commented, "Doobie Brothers! Yeah!" Mike replied, one thing led to another, and Glen and Mike got together and a business opportunity developed. Neither had seen the other in five years.

Choose Your Frequency and Style

We talked about the problem of following high-volume people. You need to decide for yourself how much you will communicate on social media, and what topics you'll address.

One thing that our marketing brothers tend to get wrong about social media is not understanding that it's not direct mail; it's not advertising; it's not TV. More is not necessarily better. Marketers who see social media as just another channel to push out messages are getting it wrong. Sure, spewing can give you a desired result, but it also can create a backlash. People are already bombarded with messaging. They may not respond to yours.

So what's your style? We recommend that you concentrate on prospects' problems in your messaging, not how great you and your company are.

You may need to feel your way here at first before you hit on the right style and the right amount of social media messaging. There's more on messaging in a subsequent section.

Get Your Messaging Straight

We talked a little about messaging in the *Perfecting Your Message* section on page 35, now it's time to get serious about the message and your approach.

You Won't Be Perfect

In your first 30 days on social media you're likely to make some mistakes. Those mistakes are likely to involve your messaging. It's OK to screw up on social media as long as you own up to your mistakes and don't offer "I apologize if anyone was offended" kinds of evasive apologies. If you're authentic, and if you **Be a Person,** you'll survive.

Among your first tasks will be to start to connect with people on social media. And that inevitably will involve meeting requests, so that's the first kind of messaging we'll examine in this section.

How to Do Meeting Requests

As your network grows and your online relationships deepen, you'll get to the point where you want a real-world meeting. We go over our plan for advancing relationships to this point in a later section. Right now, we'll concentrate on the endgame: the meeting request.

Here are two examples involving a job search — which, after all, is just a very personalized sales campaign — and a clueless networking sales request.

Gordon was looking for his next gig. He searched on LinkedIn to find target companies and executives and targeted a VP of business development for company that looked interesting. Gordon looked at the man's profile and saw he also used to work at BigERPCo. Gordon also noticed that the two of them had a lot of mutual connections. He picked the most relevant and sent the VP a message on LinkedIn.

> My name is Gordon Jackson and I'm reaching out to you to introduce myself. We have a mutual connection in Steve Smith. Like yourself I used to work at BigERPCo as well [sic], I worked almost exclusively with retailers and consumer package good companies throughout the US while I was at BigERPCo. I sold *all all* [sic] aspects of ERP software, and other software in all aspects of enterprises, financials, HR, supply chain, transportation, etc. After that, I left BigERPCo *to do to a* [sic] small boutique consulting firm around project, program, and portfolio management.

The reason for this introduction is that I wanted to see if you'd be available at some point for coffee or phone call. I'm currently looking at my career options and have heard great things about your company both while at BigERPCo and from some current employees. Andrew Jones is a friend of mine and has been telling me how great your company is. I know you have several sales positions open and with my background in software and consulting, I think I may be a good fit for your company. Let me know what your availability is for getting together and we'll go from there. I have listed my contact information below. If you'd like a copy of my resume, I can send that over to you as well. I'm looking forward to hearing from you, have a great day.

Gordon began work for that company a month later, in late 2010, in the midst of a horrible economy, and despite the two terrible typos (italicized) and other problems in his introductory message.

OK, so Gordon didn't take our advice on proofreading and no typos, but he got the interview despite the fact that everyone says that you're out on your first grammatical mistake.

So Gordon scored on the online version of a cold call. Why? First off, he referenced a mutual acquaintance, which he found out about because he did his research. His research also taught him a lot about the company and its needs, so he tailored his pitch to the company's problems, and presented his background which showed how he was the solution.

He wasn't pushy, but evidenced a tone that showed he was confident the VP would take a meeting with him. He did not oversell, claiming to be the best thing since sliced bread, and he used a conversational tone. Plus, he kept it short, making it more likely that the busy VP would read the message.

How Not to Do Meeting Requests

Our next example involves Ramesh, who's a recruiter for a consulting company. He sent our buddy Nancy a connection request on LinkedIn, saying he was a friend.

By the way, sending requests claiming to be a friend is an annoying recent trend on LinkedIn. This can rub people the wrong way, and it certainly annoyed Mike, until he figured out LinkedIn changed the default connection request to say you are a friend. Take the time to visit the profile of a target person, use the connect button, select how you know the person, and add a personal note (not the default blurb).

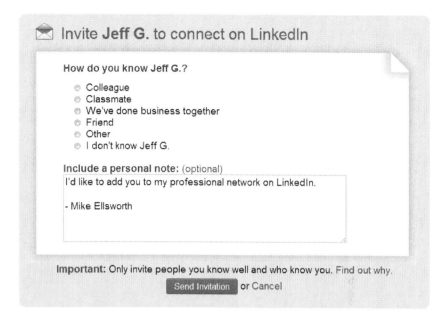

Figure 12 — Always Indicate How You Know Someone on LinkedIn

So anyway, here's the message that Ramesh sent Nancy:

> I work Downtown and would like to grow my professional network. I'd like to add you on LinkedIn.

Ramesh offers a pretty weak reason to connect. It's not likely that Nancy is interested in connecting to everyone who works downtown. She is interested in growing her network, but Ramesh doesn't give any information about what his business is or what he does. Despite the skeletal information Ramesh offered and the fact that this stranger was claiming to be a friend, Nancy accepted the connection. Shortly thereafter, Ramesh wrote:

> Nancy,
> Thanks for the LinkedIn add. Are you available to get together for coffee early next week? Monday, Tuesday, and Wednesday at 9am or 10am would work well. Any of those times work for you? Have a great day!

Ramesh still hasn't identified himself, although Nancy did check out his profile. Ramesh hasn't yet indicated why he wants to connect. After figuring out a good time, the two met. And it was like the date from hell. After 10 minutes of pleasantries, Ramesh went in for the kill: "Can you introduce me to your HR person?" Nancy said no. "Can you introduce me to any of your hiring managers?" Nancy said no.

Ramesh sat silently for a minute, then changed the subject for a few minutes. As they were wrapping up, he said, almost as an afterthought, "Can you give me a tour of your building?" Since it was almost 5 o'clock, Nancy said, "You mean after hours?" "No," said Ramesh, "in the morning." Nancy could just see that tour, with Ramesh rubbernecking at all the office nameplates and memorizing the names and titles so he could pester the managers.

"Sorry, Ramesh," Nancy said. "That's not going to happen."

Ramesh's approach was wrong in so many ways it's hard to enumerate them, but his first mistake was not revealing his intentions from the start. If he had said to Nancy, "I'm looking to get introduced to people who could benefit from the talent I represent," that still wouldn't have worked. Why? Despite the fact that Nancy would have gotten a spiff from her company if Ramesh placed an employee, she didn't know Ramesh. There was no relationship, and Nancy wasn't taking the chance of Ramesh annoying the heck out of her peers.

If you approach developing relationships via social media in the wrong way, you could come to the conclusion that social networking doesn't work, as an engineer Mike met insisted.

Mike had just finished leading a free session on using social media for job search when the engineer — let's call him Joe — approached him. "LinkedIn doesn't work for job search," he said. "Really," Mike said. "Why do you say that?" Joe proceeded to tell his sad story. He had sent a connection request to an employee of one of his target companies. The lady accepted the request. Immediately, Joe sent her an email asking that she introduce him to the hiring manager. She declined. Joe persisted, asking why she wouldn't help him. "Because I don't know you," she replied. Joe kept after her and she broke off the connection.

You may meet sales people who have the same opinion as Joe. Rest assured that, if done the right way, social media works just fine for B2B sales.

Structure Your Messages

We have developed the following structure for introductory messages. We suggest you use it whenever asking to connect via social media.

- Greeting
- Introduction
- Reference of Mutual Acquaintances/Connections
- Reference to Mutual Organizations, Clubs, and so on

- How you've helped other organizations like them
- Brief description of the BUSINESS problem you'd like to help them solve
- Next steps with them (meeting, conference call, seminar, and so on)
- Time frame
- Small request (connect on LinkedIn, talk while at an upcoming conference, and so forth)
- Give your contact information (including social media)

Those are a lot of points to hit, and you've got to keep the request short, no more than two paragraphs. So you'll have to practice until you can get the hang of it.

When you do land a meeting, don't bring brochures. Don't bring a deck. Don't send info before the meeting, except to give a link to your Website. Prepare to have a conversation.

Follow this structure and you'll be more successful than Ramesh and Joe.

Sign Up on LinkedIn

Why should you be on LinkedIn? We'll give you just one anecdote that demonstrates the power of this business-oriented social network.

But first, a quick definition: An InMail is a direct email within LinkedIn. It enables you to message people who are not in your network. Free accounts can pay for them; recruiter accounts can have an unlimited number.

Robbie got an InMail from the SVP of Talent Acquisition with BigWMS; let's call him Les. Les wrote, "I came across your profile on LinkedIn and I'm really interested in getting in touch with you because I think you'd be a good addition to our team."

Robbie replied that he wasn't looking at the time, but had great respect for the organization and you never know what could change. He continued, "I think we should get connected. On a side note, I am really interested in BigWMS from a partnership standpoint. I'm not sure who to talk to over there about this. Would you be able to help me out?"

The guy connected on LinkedIn and sent Robbie a reply. "Why don't you send me a blurb on your company and I'll make sure the right people get a hold of it."

Robbie took a recruiter and turned him into an evangelist. And landed a partnership.

Setting the Stage

In any game, there's an ante, the various capabilities and preparations you need to make yourself ready. In social media B2B sales, getting on LinkedIn is part of the ante. But just being signed up on the site is not enough. Here's how to set the stage for success on LinkedIn.

- **Have a complete LinkedIn profile (as complete as possible)** LinkedIn says that users with complete profiles are 40 times more likely to receive opportunities through LinkedIn.[77] You can check to see if your profile is complete by editing it. There's a bar in the right column towards the top that indicates completeness. The top three reasons why your profile is not complete are:

  » **No picture** — Always have a picture, of you only, professionally done. If you're sensitive about your appearance, substitute a company logo, a high school yearbook portrait, or a caricature or avatar. (There are plenty of free sites to create one.) Note: LinkedIn's terms of service do specify that only a head shot of you can be used. This rule is widely ignored, but you could get in trouble for it, so, word to the wise.

  » **No recommendations** — Ask your past and current colleagues, customers, or vendors to recommend you. You'd be surprised at the importance a short recommendation can hold. Potential partners or prospects are likely to check out your profile when considering doing business with you. A buddy of Mike's recently sealed the deal on a job offer when the employer checked out his recommendations.

  » **No skills** — LinkedIn added a skills area that enables you to list the things you're good at. Use Google (precede your search with the term "site:LinkedIn.com" to limit your search to just LinkedIn) or LinkedIn's search to find others like yourself and see what they're putting in this area. You'll want to mimic the more-successful profiles.

- **Create a company profile** Just like having a business card, a professional email account or a sign over a storefront, having a business profile on LinkedIn lends legitimacy (despite the fact that anyone can create one). If your company does not already have a company profile, be sure to check with your marketing colleagues before creating one.

---

77 LinkedIn on complete profiles: bit.ly/dtH4TT

Anyone can create a company profile, but it's important that the first person to do so for your enterprise has registered using the organization's email address. LinkedIn will search for other LinkedIn members that have similar email addresses (the part after the @ sign), so if you've registered with LinkedIn using a Gmail or other non-organizational email, get somebody else to create your enterprise's profile.

Figure 13 —Sample Company Profile on LinkedIn

After you enter a description of your enterprise, LinkedIn does a lot of work for you. They list:

• All current and former staff members on LinkedIn	• Related companies
• Employee career paths	• Common job titles — derived from employees on LinkedIn
• New hires	• Recent Promotions and Changes
• Recent Activity	• Industry
• Headquarters	• Status
• Type	• Founded
• Size	• Top Schools (of LinkedIn members)
• Website	• Jobs and recruiters

Having all this information available on LinkedIn can be a big help in finding partners and prospects. And it's free.

- **Start connecting**—You'll want to start with folks you know well in real life, like your friends, classmates, friends of your parents, alumni groups, school, church. Make each invite personal — don't use the default blurb — and easy to reference for the receiver, who may not have seen or heard from you in years.

You also may want to find out which of your contacts are already on LinkedIn. You can upload your address book from the major email services and send out invites, but resist the temptation to spam everyone you've ever met. That happened to Mike when he first joined LinkedIn, six weeks after it was founded in 2003 (he's member number 8893). Mike checked the wrong box, and sent LinkedIn invites to his 3,000 contacts. It actually turned out OK, because Mike heard back from a lot of people he hadn't talked to in a while, but he sure apologized a lot.

In addition to loading your email address book into LinkedIn, you can also upload contacts from other contact managers such as ACT![78] and even Salesforce.com.[79]

- **Connect with 3-5 LIONs**—There are some people on LinkedIn who think it's all about the numbers, and they keep score by amassing hundreds or thousands of connections. Those who will indiscriminately connect with anyone are called LIONs.

LION™ stands for LinkedIn Open Networker. LIONs are not endorsed or supported by LinkedIn. In fact, the LION concept — connect indiscriminately — runs counter to LinkedIn's slogan: Relationships Matter. Nobody knows for sure, but there are probably well in excess of 16,000 LION members on the site.

LIONs connect with anyone. They don't care who you are, what you do, what they can do for you, or what you can do for them. They tend to crow that their networks are huge. But what does a huge network of people you don't know do for you?

We're about as likely to get help with a problem, or get referred to a valuable contact, by randomly dialing the phone as we would by using a LION's network.

There is an upper limit to LIONs' — and any member's — number of connections. In 2009, when LinkedIn had only 35 million members, the service set a connection limit at 30,000. You may find some members with more, and that's probably because they had more than 30,000 connections before the limit was set. Our discussions with LIONs indicate that lots of LinkedIn account functions slow down dramatically with 30K connections.

Another limit you need to be careful of: You only are permitted 3,000 connection invitations, lifetime. That's why you'll see so many LIONs requesting that you send them an invite, rather than them inviting you.

A better strategy than being a LION is to connect with three to five relevant LIONs (make sure they have 20,000+ connections, are within your geographic area, and in your industry). By doing so, you expand you network but don't have to spend the hours a week LIONs spend just responding to connection requests.

---

78 LinkedIn's *Creating and Uploading a Contacts File*: linkd.in/tfyZO7
79 Aereus' *How to export contacts from Salesforce.com*: bit.ly/t8kIgY

- **Follow your connections' streams**—Most social networks have a newsfeed, or stream, or some constantly-updating feed of posts from your connections. LinkedIn is no exception. Your stream contains the posts and other activities of your connections, and it appears on your main LinkedIn page. Make it a habit to check out your stream at least daily.

  If you see something of interest in your stream, comment on it. It brings you to the attention of the connection who posted, and may start a dialog. Use a contact's update as an excuse to reach out to them and comment. Remember, social media is about creating relationships, not bombarding people with commercial messages. Never spam your contacts with a sales pitch.

- **Offer value via status updates**—By the same token, everything you do on LinkedIn appears on your connections' streams. So make sure you post interesting things on a regular basis with information about what you're working on or your take on current industry events and so forth. This causes you to appear in your connections' timelines, keeping them (and their connections who read their timelines) informed of what you're doing in a subtle way. One thing to consider is hooking your Twitter and Facebook account updates to your LinkedIn feed. This can get to be irritating, especially with Twitter, if you really post a lot of updates, so be careful about this.

- **Ask your connections to introduce you**—If you find people on LinkedIn you'd like to connect with, you can ask your connections to connect you. Back in the day, this used to be the only way you could connect on LinkedIn. It's still a very powerful way.

  You've probably heard of the trivia game, *Six Degrees of Kevin Bacon*. The game is based on a concept that everyone in the world is no more than six friend-of-a-friend jumps away from any other person. A scholarly study actually determined that people in the United States were no more than three degrees of separation away from one another.[80] There's no telling if this study gave birth to LinkedIn's three-tiered networking policy, but regardless, that's how the site defines the size of your network.

  People you are directly connected to are your First Degree network. When you visit their profiles or see them listed in a search, their names are followed by a 1st icon.

  Your First Degree contacts obviously also have connections. These secondary connections are your Second Degree network, denoted by a 2nd icon. You can connect to these Second Degree folks by passing a connection request through

---

80 Stanley Milgram's Small World experiment: bit.ly/crdJBb

one of your First Degree connections. That First Degree connection can decide whether or not to pass on the request, and you'll be none the wiser. If the request is passed on, the Second Degree contact is free to accept or reject the request just as if it had come from any other source. Obviously the number of people in your Second Degree network is larger than your First Degree population.

The Second Degree connections have connections themselves, and this is the limit of your addressable network: your Third Degree network. Just as with the Second Degree connections, you can pass a connection request along to a Third Degree by first passing it to a First Degree contact, who must decide to pass it to the Second Degree connection, who similarly must decide to pass it to the Third Degree connection. Confused yet?

When you add up all the people in your First, Second, and Third Degree networks, you have your total addressable network. Depending on the number of contacts each member in your addressable network has, you might be surprised at how many people you can be potentially connected to.

We recommend that when you want to contact someone you don't know at all that you use this method of passing your request through your network. Examine the target's profile. On the right side, it will tell you how you're connected through the three-degree network. Pick out a first degree connection and then select the Get introduced through a connection link on the target's profile. You see something like the following:

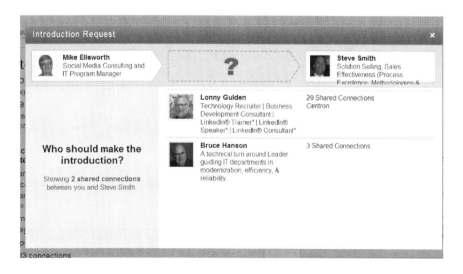

Select the connection you think is most likely to refer you on. It's like the difference between cold calling someone (like Ramesh did in our example) and getting introduced — being passed through a presumably trusted member of the target person's network implies a similar endorsement.

- **Send a LinkedIn connection invitation after meetings**—Make a habit of sending along a LinkedIn invitation to prospects after sales meetings. You certainly have a good excuse to connect. You will be fresh in their minds, and they will be more likely to connect with you right away. If they don't respond, though, don't push it.

It's also a good idea to look your prospects up on LinkedIn before the meeting, to learn more about them.

If you can't find them on LinkedIn, this is a good excuse to either bring up LinkedIn in the meeting or email them afterward and ask, "I wanted to connect with you but couldn't find you on LinkedIn. If you don't belong, I'd be happy to discuss the benefits of joining and help you get started." If they take you up on the offer, you've already expanded your relationship with them. Even if they engage you to tell you why they think LinkedIn is a waste of time and energy, you've connected with them on a new level.

If your customer or prospect does connect with you, now you will (usually) be able to see their first order network. In that network there may be connections you have in common, and you can appeal to them for ideas on how to close your prospect or delight your customer.

Also in their network you may find people who have hundreds of connections whom you might benefit from connecting to.

- **Join LinkedIn Groups**—There is a LinkedIn Group for every conceivable interest under the sun. You can join 50 at a time, so be wise about those you choose. The cool thing about groups is that you can message fellow group members, either publicly by commenting on their posts, or privately. Join 10-15 groups that are relevant to you (alumni, executive groups, groups relevant to your industry, etc). Avoid political or religious groups because you don't want to give a prospect any reason to not want to connect with you. People who belong to LinkedIn groups are generally looking to connect.

The above represent good target activities for your first 30 days. You may be impatient and think that you want to charge on to the next chapter, but we recommend against that unless you've got significant social media experience.

Why? Because, like arriving in any new country, you need to get the lay of the land. Social media is a powerful tool, and you can inadvertently hurt your cause if you don't understand how to use it. See our previous section, *Be Careful Out There!* on page 83 for some cautionary tales.

We recommend spending a month or even more on these initial steps before going on to the next chapter.

Here's our overall approach in a nutshell. Perhaps reading through it you can see why you need to spend this initial period just listening.

Social Media Performance Group Social Media Approach

Social Media Performance Group's approach involves five action verbs for execution (FAVEs) that you should keep in mind as you begin to engage with your community.

Listen

This one's first for a reason. Many sales people forget that you must listen before you speak. You must offer before you take. You must engage before you ask for action. Spend the first month or more of your social computing engagement process just listening to what people are saying. Restrain yourself from responding, even (especially!) if you see things you don't like. Gauge the tenor of the conversation. What words do they use? How are they feeling? What gets them upset? What goads them to action?

During this phase, follow the old adage: It is better to be silent and thought a fool than to open your mouth and remove all doubt.

While you're listening, start sorting your community into segments. Who are the loudmouths? Who are respected? Who are emotional about your product? Who are skeptical?

You'll want to devise different approaches to the groups you find. The beauty of social computing is it enables you to address different groups differently. Start planning your engagement strategy while you listen.

Find

OK this one logically comes first. How can you listen until you find who's speaking? But we hope you see why Listen has to come first.

Mark Zuckerberg, the young creator of Facebook, famously said, "Communities already exist. Instead, think about how you can help that community do what it wants to do."

There's a community out there talking about you or your business. You need to find it and engage with it. Help it do what it wants to do. You probably won't have to look hard, but you should realize the community may exist only online, only offline, or both. If it's only offline, you've got a bit of convincing to do to get them online.

To find your community, ask around. Ask others in your field. Google your business, products, product category. Search on LinkedIn.

Engage

Engaging with your community means — at last! — joining the ongoing conversation. Don't think that you can land like a ton of bricks and start dominating. Follow the 4-to-1 rule: Comment on four posts for every post that you write. Give — invest — in the relationship before you ask for anything.

See the examples of Joe the engineer who insisted social networking didn't work on page 116 and hapless Ramesh's clumsy approach on page 114.

So what our Ramesh and Joe didn't realize, and what you need to always keep in mind, is that it's **social** networking. Approach it as you would approach building a relationship in real life. You may be able to meet more people online, but they're still people, and will develop a relationship with you over time, not immediately.

Ask

After you've earned your stripes with your community or a prospect, you can start asking for action. Your first Ask shouldn't be as bold as, "By our product," or "Give us your number and a sales person will call." You've just met these people! It would be like arriving at a party in a beautiful mansion and asking, "So how much did you pay for this dump, anyway?" You could say that to your best friend, but you aren't best friends with your community yet.

We don't necessarily recommend that you ask at all! Using our approach, you may never have to, but there's more on that in a later section. If you do ask, make sure your Ask is appropriate to the reputation and amount of social capital you've amassed through your participation. By no means should you immediately set up your own community and ask everyone to join. That step comes later, much later, if ever, and you'll probably know when it's appropriate.

Measure

You'll read a lot about social computing measurement on the Web. It's an obsession among certain people, many of whom swear it's not possible to measure social media outcomes.

We think social media is the only medium where it is possible to measure outcomes exactly.

You'll hear people claim, "I know exactly how many sales I'll get if I do this direct mail campaign." And they may be right. Through trial and error, they've discovered an approach that works. But can they tell you which of their messages go immediately into recycling? No, because if they could, they wouldn't mail those pieces out in the first place.

It's the same with TV and radio advertising. It's an old saw in the advertising world: "I know half of what I spend on advertising is wasted. I just don't know which half." Heh. Not really that funny considering you're talking blithely about wasting more than $209 billion annually in the US alone.

Online you can connect your actions with the response. Don't let anyone tell you any differently. It may not be a snap to do, but it is possible.

Your First 60 Days on Social Media

To me, business is all P2P: people to people.
Social media is about consistently sharing
valuable, timely, relevant content with the right audience,
engaging with your networks,
and fostering relationships.

Mari Smith
social media speaker, author

Now that you've spent your first 30 days on social media, concentrating on LinkedIn, it's time to branch out a bit. You're still not ready to get really engaged, but you'll get there at the end of this month.

Tasks for this month include:

Familiarize yourself with the social media sites listed in the Social Sites Defined chapter

- Learn advanced search on LinkedIn

- Learn to search LinkedIn on Google

- Start connecting with your groups

- Visit LinkedIn daily

- Start paying attention to who searched you

- Get on Twitter and start following people

Familiarize Yourself with Social Media Sites

We gave you a quick overview of some interesting social media sites in the Social Sites Defined chapter. As part of your first 60 days, you should visit each of them and, by doing a little keyword searching, determine whether your community is there, and participating.

You for sure need to get on LinkedIn, which we hope you did during your first 30 days. But whether you can be effective on Twitter, Facebook, and YouTube is something you should determine.

Your first task is to take a look at several other social media sites, beyond LinkedIn. You may feel that LinkedIn, with its emphasis on business, is the only site you need, and you could be right. But you could also miss out on tremendous opportunities to connect with your community by only focusing on LinkedIn.

At this writing, the top social media sites, in descending order of number of users, are:[81]

Social Networking Site	Number of Members (millions, June 2012)
Facebook	901
Twitter	555
Google+	170
LinkedIn	150
Pinterest	11.7

Pinterest is the new kid on the block, and came out of nowhere over a few months at the end of 2011, and in January 2012, became the fastest in history to break the 10 million unique viewers mark. Almost as new is Google+, which started in mid-2011 and has experienced phenomenal growth.

However, the number of users is not the only metric you should consider when thinking about where to spend your social media time. Time spent per month may be more important. Take a look at how using this measure changes the ranking of sites: [82]

81 Social Media and Social Good's *User Activity Comparison Of Popular Social Networking Sites*: bit.ly/KPmpY7
82 Marketing Ideas 101's *Social Media: Average Time Spent*: bit.ly/KZznAJ (January 2012)

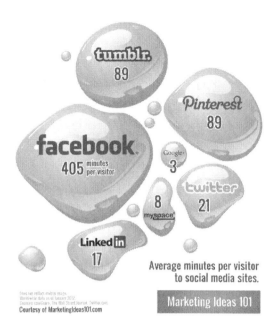

Average minutes per visitor
to social media sites.

Marketing Ideas 101

Courtesy of MarketingIdeas101.com

Social Networking Site	Time Spent per month (in Minutes)
Facebook	405
Tumblr	89
Pinterest	89
Twitter	21
LinkedIn	17
MySpace	8
Google+	3

Wow. Even fading, crusty, old MySpace beats new kid Google+! You may not recognize the site Tumblr. It's an up-and-coming blogging site, and it's tied with the new darling, Pinterest, in user engagement.

But look at LinkedIn. On average, users only spend 17 minutes a month on the site.

Perhaps now you understand the need to branch out a bit from LinkedIn. Good choices are Twitter — the billboard of social media sites — and Facebook — the 901 pound gorilla. But you might also consider Tumblr, and even think about writing a blog. But we'll get to that in a later section.

We recommend that you at least check out all the sites we mentioned in the Social Sites Defined chapter. And we really recommend signing up for Facebook, Twitter, and one site not mentioned in the lists above: YouTube.

Why YouTube?

Because videos, especially how-to videos, are a great way to reach your prospects. Talk to your marketing folks about creating a series of low-cost problem-solving videos. We're not talking about high-end, customer testimonial, slick pieces. We're talking down and dirty short videos that solve customer problems or demonstrate how to use your product. If you sell services, creating customer case study videos can be quite effective, especially if they go into details about how they used your services to solve a problem.

One of our prospects paid big bucks to have an ad agency make a series of client testimonial videos. These productions had multiple camera views, tracking shots, graphics that zoomed in and out, and the clients were well-spoken and convincing.

The client posted the glossy vids on YouTube and promoted them on their blog. The result: Over a six-month period, the 12 videos in aggregate had fewer than 1,200 views. One video had three views, and two of them were from us! The company probably dropped $120,000 on the package, yielding an outlay of $100 per view. You'd do better handing out C-notes on street corners.

Contrast that with a company like Blendtec, which we talked about back on page 85, and which, for very little money, created a viral sensation by destroying things in its blender.

Lest you get the idea that YouTube is only for B2C, take a look at what Kinaxis, a supply chain risk management company, did with their Suitemates series on YouTube and on its own Website, www.suitemates.com.[83]

True, the production values are high, and the actors are recognizable, but the story makes supply chain risk management sound fascinating. The Canadian company's tagline for the series — The Series BigERP Doesn't Want You to Watch — was intriguing and compelling. It's worth taking a look at their case study[84]

---

83 *Suitemates by Kinaxis: Ep-1 - Two Peas in a Prison:* bit.ly/Ncf2wP
84 TellAllMarketing's *B2B Case Study: How Kinaxis Uses Social Media*: bit.ly/MCaajJ

to see how they brought all the elements of social media and search engine optimization together.

We especially like this case study because it features Kinexis' community, the Supply Chain Expert Community.[85]

According to the case study, Kinexis experienced:

- 2.7X increase in traffic to Kinaxis.com

- 3.2X increase in conversions (leads closed)

- 5.3X increase in traffic to the blog/community, which now numbers more than 6,000 users, 75 percent of which are non-customers

- Double-digit subscription growth for its SaaS (Software as a Service) product RapidResponse to more than 30,000 users

Hey, did you catch that bit about tripling leads closed and that three-quarters of their community members are not customers (AKA prospects)? Here's real-world proof that the stuff we've been telling you works!

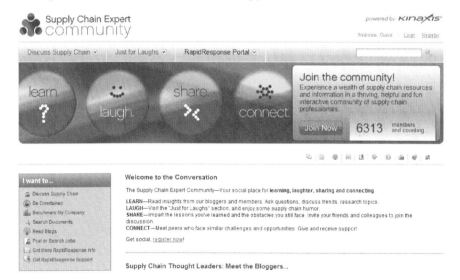

Figure 14 — Kinaxis' Supply Chain Expert Community

---

85 Kinaxis' *Supply Chain Expert Community*: bit.ly/LhM3Y4

The lesson here is there is more to social media than LinkedIn, and there's more to a social media strategy than posting once in a while on various social networks.

If you want to take a look at some award-winning videos to get a feel of what's possible, read about the Beagle Research Group's 2011 Short Tale Awards. [86]

Learn Advanced Search on LinkedIn

LinkedIn's regular search is OK. It lets you search members, updates, jobs, companies, groups and LinkedIn Answers (more on that feature later). However, all searching using the free account is limited to just 100 results, so you'll want to narrow your search to ensure that what turns up is relevant.

Well, the good news is there are lots of advanced search features. The bad news is that some of the most useful require you to upgrade to a paid account.

Using LinkedIn's advanced search, you can zero in on relevant members you might want to connect with. Despite the fact that some of the most interesting and powerful search fields are reserved for use by premium members, take a look at the advanced search form and we think you'll agree; it's still pretty powerful. For example, you can search for current employees only to get more granular and relevant results.

---

86 Beagle Research Group's *Short Tale Award 2011*: bit.ly/MEqKM7

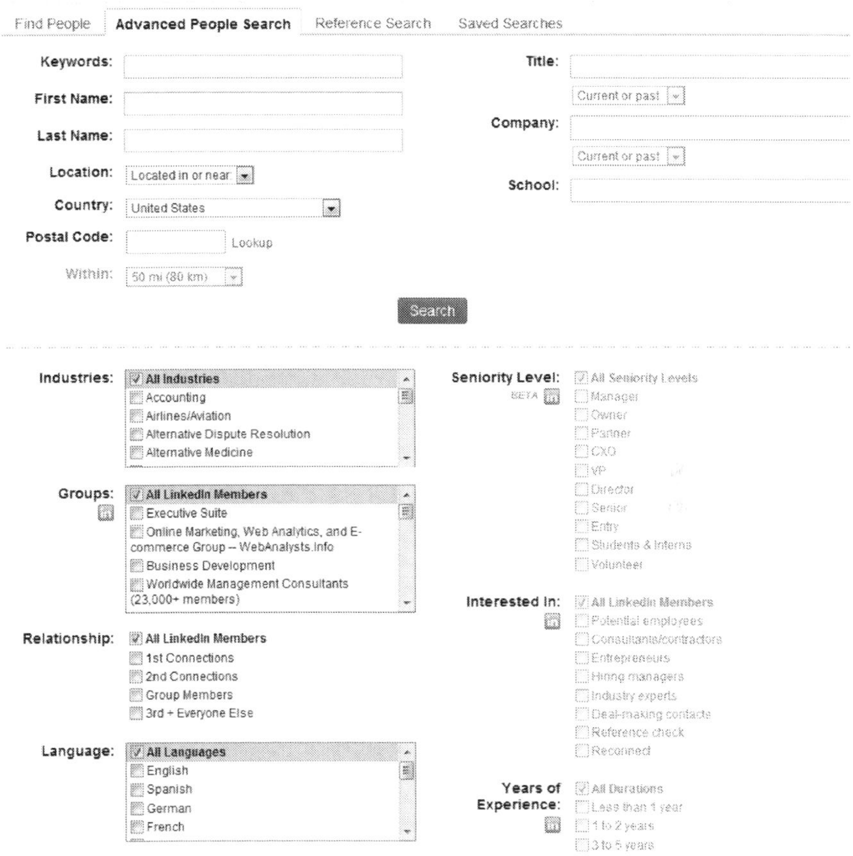

Figure 15 — LinkedIn Advanced Search Page

The various grayed-out areas are only available to premium accounts. You can still search by industry, language, location, title, company, and school, however, for free. Of course, if you want to use Google as your search engine, as we've briefly mentioned before, you may be able to get at some of the premium attributes, and get way more than 100 results.

If you think paying for LinkedIn premium accounts is for you, here are the current increases in the number of results you can see for each account type:

- Upgrade to a Business Account ($19.95/month) to see 300 results at a time

- Upgrade to a Business Plus Account ($39.95/month) to see 500 results at a time

- Upgrade to a Pro Account (AKA Executive Account **$74.95**/month) to see **700 results** at a time

Seventy-five bucks to see just 700 results? Hardly seems worth it. For this reason, we recommend learning a few Google searching tricks.

Learn How to Search LinkedIn on Google

An alternative to paying for better LinkedIn search is to use Google, which places no limits on the number of search results. To get started, simply format your Google query like either of the following:

site:linkedin.com +<name of your industry> +CEO +<your location>

site:linkedin.com +<name of your industry > +"business deals" +<your location>

For example, the following query recently turned up 1,480 results — 14X the number you could get with the free LinkedIn account:

site:linkedin.com allintext: CEO Minneapolis "medical device"

As we've covered briefly before, the "site:" modifier restricts the Google search to pages on the target site, in this case, LinkedIn. The "allintext:" modifier means to ignore keywords that don't appear in the text of the page — for example, those that appear in the title or the URL. There are lots of other modifiers you can use with advanced Google searching as well, such as using a plus sign to indicate the keyword is required or a minus sign to omit a keyword from the search.

If you can't remember the arcane modifiers, simply select Advanced Search from the bottom of any Google page, and you'll see a form that helps you build your query:

Google

Advanced Search

Find pages with...

all these words:	CEO Minneapolis
this exact word or phrase:	medical device
any of these words:	
none of these words:	
numbers ranging from:	to

Then narrow your results by...

language:	any language
region:	any region
last update:	anytime
site or domain:	linkedin.com
terms appearing:	in the text of the page
SafeSearch:	off moderate strict
reading level:	no reading level displayed
file type:	any format
usage rights:	not filtered by license

Figure 16 — Google's Advanced Search Form

Remember, however, Google search is limited to LinkedIn members' public profiles, while the internal search looks at all member information.

Here's a more-advanced example of a Google search of LinkedIn:

site:www.linkedin.com   -inurl:answers   -inurl:jobs   -inurl:companies -inurl:directory YOUR KEYWORDS HERE

Let's take a look at this example bit by bit:

- **site**: — Use this keyword to restrict Google's search to a particular site, in this case, LinkedIn

- **-inurl**: — This keyword, combined with the minus sign, excludes pages with certain keywords in the URL. In this case, we don't want to see results from the LinkedIn Answers section, the Jobs section, the company pages or company directory. If you do want to see answers in a specific section, change the minus sign to a plus sign.

- **Keywords** — put your keywords, using plus, minus, quotes, or AND or OR to further qualify the search

For example, this search:

> **site:www.linkedin.com -inurl:answers -inurl:jobs -inurl:companies -inurl:directory "project manager"**

finds four million project managers on LinkedIn. That's far better than the 100 search results the free LinkedIn account limits you to.

One final tip: You may find it useful to use Google to search for people with a particular number of LinkedIn recommendations. These people are likely to be highly connected and thus good candidates to help you build your network. The following search produces a list of 600,000 highly-recommended LinkedIn users:

> **site:linkedin.com +"6 people have recommended"**

We restrict the search to only the LinkedIn site and we ensure only people with six recommendations are found using the plus sign with the phrase "6 people have recommended."

Use Google to Evaluate Social Media Sites

To determine which social sites will be the most productive use of your time, you need to find where your prospects and customers already are on social media, and then be there. To do this, start out with some Google searches.

To use Google to find your community, first do a little thinking about the keywords that community members are likely to use.

For example, if your product category is small business accounting software, Google that term.[87] Currently, that search, without quotes, yields more than 37 million results. OK, that's a bit hard to put your arms around. If you try the term as a phrase, by surrounding it with quotes, you get under 21,000 results.[88] That may seem a bit more manageable, but it still may not give the results you can use to locate places where your community is talking.

Incidentally, you'll notice when you type a search string into Google, a little window drops down from the entry area with suggestions for similar searches and Google instantly shows you results based on what it thinks you're looking for. You also may notice that after you do a search, little ads — called AdWords — appear on the right side of the search results. Refer to the next figure to see what we mean.

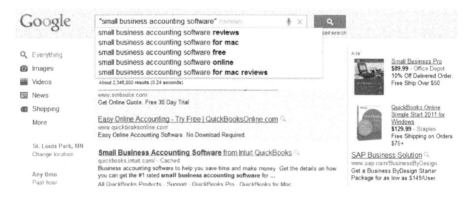

Figure 17 — Google Query with AdWords Sidebar — Example

You may find the search suggestions Google offers interesting. If not, be sure to take a look at the AdWords on the right side. These organizations might be worth investigating, as they could be competitors or potential partners, and visiting their sites may give you ideas for how to find your community online.

Be aware that each time you click on an AdWord, somebody pays Google some money, from cents to dozens of dollars. If that bothers you, you can copy the Web address from the AdWord into your browser's address bar and visit the site for free.

---

87 Google search for small business accounting software, with no quotes: bit.ly/poUVZM
88 Google search for small business accounting software, with quotes: bit.ly/LdITqj

Back to our example. What you really want to do is to find people talking about small business accounting software on social media sites. So one thing you can do is to restrict your search to certain social media sites adding a qualifier like:

site:facebook.com

Adding site:facebook.com to the Google query we're working on produces 3,800 results. OK, now we're getting somewhere. Here's what we got when we ran that search:

Figure 18 — Restricting a Google Search to Facebook Only

From these results we can see that people are indeed talking about small business accounting software on Facebook. Following the various links yields a group entitled "DIY Tax Accounting Software group," with more than a hundred members. If you make small business accounting software, you've just found a potential place to engage with your community.

You can repeat this exercise with other social media sites. Doing it with LinkedIn yields 717 people you'd probably like to know. Doing it with Twitter yields more than 3,000 posts. Doing it with YouTube produces more than 1,500 links to videos.

You get the picture. Google is your friend, and using the site qualifier — and other advanced features — you can tailor a search to find where your community is talking.

Advanced Google Searching

No matter what you're searching for, you should be sure to check out Google's More button. It offers a wealth of ways to specialize your search, including searching for:

• Web	• Images
• Maps	• Videos
• News	• Shopping
• Books	• Places
• Blogs	• Flights
• Discussions	• Recipes
• Applications	• Patents

Clicking "Show search tools" offers you ways to restrict your search by time and type:

• Any time	• All results
• Latest	• Sites with images
• Past 24 hours	• Related searches
• Past week	• Dictionary
• Past month	• Reading level
• Past year	• Nearby
• Custom range...	• Translated foreign pages

As interesting as these options are, the one we really want to concentrate on is a relatively new one: Google's Social Search.

Once you're active in social networking, you may notice that you often see little notices below the search results, like in the following figure.

141

Figure 19 — Example of Google Social Circle Search Result

The concept that seeing results from people you know is going to be more interesting and relevant to you is called social search. Knowing that people in our social networks have written or tagged related articles might make us more likely to click on these results.

Depending on who your friends are, you might find the social search content interesting, inspiring, or insipid. Google has a nice introduction to social search on YouTube[89] that can help you better understand how it works, but the company is relatively mum about its future plans for the feature.

If you have a large online social circle and you post content relevant to your company and the business problem you solve, you are almost guaranteeing that anyone in your circle who searches for relevant terms will see your information on the first page of search results. Organizations pay hundreds to hundreds of thousands of dollars per month to get on the first page, so having a large, relevant social circle can create essentially free targeted advertising.

---

89 Google's YouTube video about social search: bit.ly/aeLBCl

Other Ways to Find Your Community

There are a variety of free tools that can help you find prospects. A good one we use is Social Mention.[90] This tool searches social media in real time to find your keywords and gives various metrics on their effectiveness.

Figure 20 - SocialMention Real-Time Search

We're not going to go through all the various measurements represented here, but we would like to draw your attention to the Sentiment numbers. These represent a best guess of the attitude expressed in all posts found, in aggregate. For the keywords we used, most mentions were neutral in nature. You'll want to use the sentiment measure to test out the keywords you'll want to use in your social media messaging. Find keywords with a high positive sentiment and your messages will likely have a larger effect.

---

90 Social Mention: bit.ly/cNFCk4

Start Connecting with Groups

During your first 30 days on social media, you joined some LinkedIn Groups. We hope you joined a bunch of relevant groups, because now you're going to start to use them to develop relationships with group members.

Before going off whole hog, though, let's take a look at the groups you joined. Are they the best groups for you? One way to find out is to do a specialized group search.

From the top bar, mouse over Groups and select Groups Directory. It may take a moment for the page to display, since at this writing, there are more than 1.3 million groups on LinkedIn.

On the left side of the page, you'll notice several selections, as in the following figure.

Figure 21 — Using the LinkedIn Groups Directory

Also notice that the directory is sorted by the number of first level connections who are members of a group. Using the checkboxes to the left, you can see only the groups that your first level connections belong to. These are probably the groups that you'll want to start mining for new connections.

You can also restrict the list to your current groups, groups LinkedIn thinks you might like, and by specifying only open groups (those that anyone can join) or members-only groups. Finally you can filter so that only groups that speak your language are listed.

Figure 22 — Filtering LinkedIn's Groups Directory

Using the filters, we've reduced the 1.3 million possible groups to 19 that our first level connections belong to and that LinkedIn thinks we might like, based on what the site knows about us. Using the View buttons next to each group, we can explore the groups and join them.

You can also search the group directory by keywords. Let's try the ones we've been using, "small business accounting software." LinkedIn returns only a single group result, and it's in Malaysia, so that's not going to work. However, keep this finding in mind for the next section, because you may want to consider starting your own group.

Removing the quotes turns up 17 results. We can now check out these groups to see if we're interested in joining them.

Group membership is a big part of the Infinite Pipeline Relationship Development Process that we detail in the next chapter. But for right now, you'll want to lurk (read posts but contribute nothing) in your groups.

We don't recommend jumping in with both feet until you've gauged the type of messages that are typical in the group. Many groups discourage or are actively hostile to self-promotion or other advertising, and some will expel members who engage in such behavior. You're there to learn, at first, and once you've got a handle on group rules and expectations, you can take the next step, which is commenting.

You may be tempted to reach out to group members at this point, but we recommend you do so cautiously. LinkedIn groups have two great networking assets:

145

- They gather together like-minded people who might be interested in what you're selling

- You can message group members directly

If you jump right to a private message to a group member asking them to meet with you or buy your stuff, you're going to flop badly.

Instead, start your interaction by Liking other peoples' posts. This gets you in front of the group and can gently initiate relationships. When you Like a post, the poster may become curious, view your profile, and may even send you a connection request. We talk about finding out who has viewed your profile in the section *Start Paying Attention to Who Searched You* on page 150.

Another thing you can do to get started is to Follow other members' activity. You'll start to get updates that the member posts. LinkedIn doesn't send emails or notifications when someone follows you, but you can always see a complete list of your followers.

To see who's following you:

1. Click **Groups** at the top of your home page.

2. Click the group's name.

3. Click **More** in the row under your group's name and then select **Your Activity**.

4. Click **(Your Name)'s Followers** on the left. If you don't have any followers, this option doesn't appear.

5. You see something like the following figure

Figure 23 — Finding Your LinkedIn Followers

Groups are one of the most powerful features of LinkedIn. Take your time and keep it on the down low until you learn the ropes. You'll learn how to really leverage their power in a later section.

Visit LinkedIn Daily

Take at least 15 minutes a day to visit LinkedIn. We know you're busy, but if you've got any time to do prospecting, carve out 15 minutes to develop your LinkedIn presence.

A good way to spend your 15 minutes is on your home page, the one you see when you first enter LinkedIn. That's where your activity feed displays.

There are several sections to the home page, and we'll go over important ones in the following.

Your Update

At the top of your page is an area for you to post an update. Use it to talk about what you're working on, offer a link to an interesting article, or post something funny. Feel free to post more than once a day, but not constantly.

Your status appears in all your connections' activity feeds, and it's a good way to stay in front of them.

The area just below the update box displays posts from Facebook or Twitter if you've enabled cross-posting from these sites. That's an advanced technique and we don't recommend it for a newbie. Also, at this writing, LinkedIn and Twitter have parted ways and it may be harder to cross-post in the future.

LinkedIn Today

LinkedIn has a nice feature that summarizes information that you may find interesting. It displays it under your status area, and also emails it to you. Consider following one of these links and reposting it in your status if you think your connections will like it.

Activity Stream

All **Updates** · Coworkers · Shares · More ▾   Recent · Top

Show 3 more recent updates...

Peter LaBore is now connected to Lance Andries, Scouting for top talent @ Target!
Send a message · 27 seconds ago

Leon E. Spencer via Twitter 🐦
leonespencer Social media helps U recruit athletes http://t.co/YH9qxjq3
☆ Favorite ⭕ Retweet ↩ Reply · 56 seconds ago

Dennis Deery is now connected to Bill Coleman, Owner, Community Technology Advisors, Executive Director of Dakota Future, Vicki Lawler Prock, Director, Network Development and Advisor Support at Galliard Group, Marie Hvidsten, Rural Leadership Specialist at NDSU and 3 other people.
Send a message · 4 minutes ago

Scott Colesworthy is now connected to Katharine Allen, Co-President, InterpretAmerica, Hide LLC and Owner at Sierra Sky Interpreting & Translation, Steve Cady, Small Business Owner & Sales Specialist, Joseph Rubin, Division President at Field Solutions, LLC and 2 other people.
Send a message · 6 minutes ago

Jacqueline (Jackie) Buck SPHR has accepted a new opportunity with the Department of Employment and Economic Development at the State of Minnesota. I will be focusing on key statewide Job Service initiatives and providing strategic leadership to the Business Services program. Looking forward to the new... more
Like · Comment · Send a message · 8 minutes ago

Figure 24 — LinkedIn Activity Stream Example

Most of your home page is taken up with updates from your connections. There are several ways you can interact with these updates, depending on the type.

- **Send a message** — When your connections make new connections or take any of several actions on LinkedIn, this information shows up in your activity feed. You can respond by sending your connection a direct message.

- **Favorite** — Posts from other social media sites often enable you to Favorite the posts. For Twitter posts, you can retweet or reply as well.

- **Like** — Changes in status and other actions enable you to Like the post. This is an especially good idea when your connection has a job status change; it's a good excuse to reconnect.

- **Comment** — Many types of statuses enable you to comment. Your connection sees the comment as well as anyone following either of you, so make your comment pungent.

As you can see, you've got plenty of ways to interact with your first-level connections. Start out simple, and don't graduate to asking for action until you've got the hang of LinkedIn.

Just Joined LinkedIn

Just joined LinkedIn

Colleagues
Social Media Performance Group
State of Minnesota
StratVantage Consulting, LLC
Linked InSolutions
Evalubase Research
Geneer
VirtualFund.com, Inc.
ACNielsen Company
A. C. Nielsen

Alumni
University of Denver
Duke University

Figure 25 — Just Joined LinkedIn Example

Below your activity feed is a very important area: listings of people who share a connection with you who recently joined LinkedIn.

This section is updated daily and lists new LinkedIn users that worked at or attended the companies and schools listed on your profile. So make sure your profile lists all your employers and schools.

Now what's the first thing a new LinkedIn user is going to want to do? That's right: Connect with other members. So even if you don't know or remember the folks in these lists, you might consider sending them a connection request, saying something like, "We both worked at XYZ Company, but I don't think we were there at the same time. I thought maybe you'd like to connect and talk about old times."

As a newbie, your potential contact is likely to welcome a friendly invitation. It's even better if you visit their profile first and in your note mention some other common interests.

Other Sections

There are other sections on your home page, but we're not going to go through them all. We will take a look at one more very important one in the next section.

Start Paying Attention to Who Searched You

Figure 26 — LinkedIn "Who's Viewed Your Profile?" Example

In the right column of your LinkedIn home page is a section that displays who has viewed your profile and how many times you appeared in search results.

Folks who have looked at your profile might be interested in talking to you, right? Click on the link and you'll see something similar to the following figure:

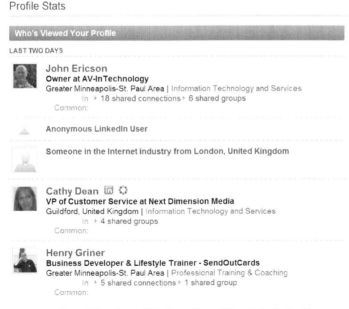

Figure 27 — People Who Have Viewed Your LinkedIn Profile

You'll notice that you can find out a lot about some of the people who have visited your profile, but next to nothing about others. This is a setting that each member can control, and with the free account, there's nothing you can do to see more information about the anonymous viewers.

For those who are identified, you can find out a lot about them: How many connections you have in common, the groups you share, and you can click their names to view their profiles.

They were looking at you so they won't necessarily be surprised if you message them in one of your shared groups. But be careful. Some people browse dozens of profiles a day (especially recruiters) and they may not remember you.

For now, ensure that you visit LinkedIn each day and carefully begin to use its various ways to communicate and connect.

Get on Twitter and Start Following People

During your various searches, participation in LinkedIn Groups and other searching for your community, you've probably developed a list of interesting people. No matter what you think of Twitter, an important step in getting to know these people, their concerns, and how they are participating on social media is to look for them on Twitter.

We sense you may need a little convincing to venture into a social network that has a reputation for insipid and meaningless blather.

OK, what would it take to convince you? How about a method for converting individual tweets (what Twitter posts are called) into $250,000 B2B contracts? That's what enterprise telecommunications firm Avaya has done.

Want to know how?

Here's their process for finding, nurturing and capturing demand: [91]

- Discover conversations that are worth having

- Converse in ways that generate questions that its products/services can answer

- Align conversations with traditional lead management processes

---

91 MakeSocialMediaSell.com's *Successful B2B use of Twitter | Avaya is aligning sales with Social* bit. ly/NaXA8q

According to MakeSocialMediaSell.com, by monitoring Twitter, Avaya's sales team came upon a tweet:

"[BigTelco] or avaya? Time for a new phone system very soon."

Social media manager Paul Dunay quickly responded:

"@[prospect] – let me know if we can help you – we have some Strategic Consultants that can help you assess your needs."

It took Dunay but moments to type those 117 characters (he could have blathered all the way to 140). But, as you know, timing is everything. Dunay was there at the moment a need was revealed, and offered to create a solution. Thirteen days later, Avaya closed a $250,000 sale.

Interested in finding a little bit more about this so-called irrelevant hipster network now?

OK, let's address that elephant in the room. It's true. Much of what is said on Twitter is trivial. There are lots of people tweeting about meaningless things. Our top worst tweets ever:

"I'm going up the stairs now" — tied with "OMG, just saw something black going up the stairs behind me, please tell me its my cat! I'm gonna be looking behind me every 10 seconds now!"

"My cat just rolled over" — tied with *MY CAT JUST ROLLED OVER* onto me… cuddle time?:3"

"Gee, the line at Starbucks is long" — tied with "What is the deal with the long drive thru line at Starbucks? My gas light is coming on people!"

So the scoffers have a bit of a point. There are plenty of self-involved people using Twitter to spout trivial inanities or unwanted details about their lives.

However, to condemn Twitter because some people say stupid things on it is like condemning the telephone network because people say stupid things on it. Both are ways for people to communicate. And both host a wide variety of conversations, some vapid, some deadly serious, and a whole lot of them are about business.

In fact, a psychographic survey conducted by the Kamaron Research Institute[92] found that more than 8 in 10 people said that at least one of the reasons that they

92 The Kamaron Institute's *The Majority of People On Twitter Tweet For Business, Poll Shows*: bit.ly/NQJePn

tweet was for business purposes. Less than two in ten (17 percent) did not list business as one of the reasons that they tweet.

So, yeah, there's lots of business being done on Twitter, including B2B business.

Since you're still new on social media, we recommend (as always) you start out on Twitter by listening. See if you can find those target prospects on the list you've been developing via LinkedIn and your Google searching. In fact, many business people list their Twitter account names right on their profiles, as in the following figure.

Figure 28 — The Follow on Twitter Button on LinkedIn

So when you find an interesting prospect on LinkedIn you can click on the Follow button even if you aren't ready yet to propose a connection. The prospect will see that you've followed them and may greet you or thank you for following. This is a great opportunity to engage, but, as you probably have guessed, it's a little too early to get selling. Instead you can reply about how much you enjoyed a recent tweet.

But to do this, you've first got to sign up for Twitter, and that's pretty painless. [93]

How to Use Twitter

When you sign up for a Twitter account, be sure to use your real name for your Twitter name (also called a handle, a remnant from the "10-4 good buddy" CB craze of the late '70s and early '80s[94]) or possibly the name of your enterprise, although Twitter officially frowns on this. If you don't use either, select a good username using keywords or a brandable phrase (15 character limit). Pick something related to your product category to better brand yourself as an expert and improve your findability.

Be sure to create your profile, which is limited to 160 characters (20 characters more than a tweet). Include information about yourself or your business, and add

93 Sign up for Twitter: bit.ly/aRhclP
94 See a definition for handle at: bit.ly/bOduGd

a picture of yourself or your logo. All this information will be publicly viewable, and searchable, which is important. Be sure to use lots of keywords (the same ones you've been developing) so people can find you when searching for common words and phrases.

Make sure you have a secure password. There have been numerous examples of bad guys taking over people's Twitter accounts due to weak passwords. A strong password is at least eight characters long; uses upper- and lowercase letters, numbers, and punctuation; and is not a single English word. This is good advice for all your social media accounts.

How to Get Twitter Followers

Since you're still a newbie, we suggest you start out on Twitter by following interesting people. Following means you will see their tweets in your timeline, similar to the following figure:

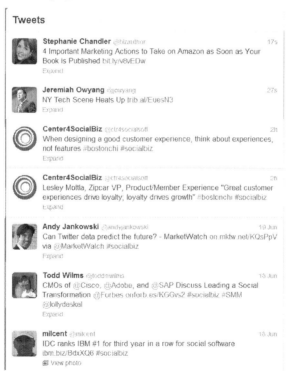

Figure 29 — Example Twitter Timeline

You can start by following us: @smpgcom, @MikeEllsworth, and @rljohnsoninc. If you know a person's Twitter handle, you can go to their page on the Web by typing twitter.com followed by a slash and their handle, without the @ sign. For example, here we are: **twitter.com/smpgcom.**

One thing you'll find out once you start following people is that you'll magically get some followers of your own. That's because not only are your tweets now showing up on your followers' sites, but many people track new followers of people they follow, and decide to also follow. In general, the more people you follow, the more will follow you back. You can find likely people to follow by searching for keywords that interest you.

Searching on Twitter

It's simple to search on the Twitter Website. At the top of your main page, you see a black toolbar like the following figure.

Figure 30 — The Twitter Toolbar

Home takes you to your Twitter feed where posts by the people you follow show up and scroll.

Click @Connect to see tweets that others have retweeted or mentioned you in as well as new people who are following you.

Click #Discover to see featured stories Twitter thinks you might be interested in.

Type a keyword you want to use to search tweets or tweeps into the entry area to the right on the toolbar. Twitter will look for tweets or people that match. Twitter searches the person's handle (@someone) as well as their profile for the keyword.

The search result will likely contain both people and tweets. You can make your search a bit more selective by using hashtags.

Searching with Hashtags

A hashtag is simply a way to tag a word as a keyword by preceding the word with a # sign (called a hash sign). Using a hashtag is a bit more specific than using a regular keyword and makes tagged tweets a little easier to find. Note that you cannot include any spaces in a hashtag.

Anyone can create a hashtag at any time. Whether anyone else uses it depends on how well-named it is, and how much you popularize it.

You may want to create or find a hashtag for your products or your enterprise.

Here's an example of a search for the hashtag #B2B:

Figure 31 — Twitter Search Using a Hashtag

When you're ready to send out your first tweet, start by saying something about what you're interested in. Just try not to make it about your cat, going up stairs, or how long the line at Starbucks is.

Incidentally, your followers are called tweeps, not twits.

Posting a Tweet

To the extreme right of the black bar on the top of your Twitter home page is a little blue and white symbol that looks like a piece of paper with a quill pen. Click that to open a form for you to post a tweet. Twitter will automatically shrink the URLs you might include in your tweet to make them shorter (like all the bit.ly URLs in our footnotes) and save space.

If you want to address your tweet to a specific person, or make sure one or more people see it on their timelines, include their handle (@somebody) in the tweet. If you want to address a tweet to a person and make it visible to anyone who visits their page and sees their timeline, don't make the @handle the first thing in the tweet. Many people make a period (.) the first character, followed directly by the @handle. There's a good Twitter cheat sheet at Makeuseof that you might want to print and study.[95]

95 Makeuseof's *Twitter CheatSheet*: bit.ly/TvoHjw

Your First 90 Days on Social Media

Pick your spots and start by doing one thing well.
For many B2B companies, blogs are the killer app
because of their long-tail search performance.
Or perhaps a vigorous LinkedIn campaign
is the ticket to create awareness of your expertise
in specific markets.
Whatever you do, don't try to boil the ocean.
Master one tool before moving on to others.
Don't spread yourself too thin.

Paul Gillin,
social media marketing author

So far in your first 60 days on social media, we've repeatedly preached caution, and listening. We've also encouraged you to build lists of keywords and prospects you'd like to get to know.

We still would like you to be cautious, especially in your messaging, but now's the time to get a lot more methodical and organized about your use of social media.

This month you'll:

- Build networking charts of companies and contacts you are targeting
- Identify prospects who use LinkedIn often
- Understand LinkedIn InMails and send some select ones to people you have never met
- Start connecting in the real world with some connections
- Use automated tools to help make usage more efficient
- Create a LinkedIn Group
- Create a blog

Build Networking Charts

You probably already do some sort of customer and prospect tracking, perhaps in a Customer Relationship Management (CRM) system. These systems are generally fine for tracking one-to-many relationships (how you are related to lots of other people). Perhaps you use the capabilities of these systems to track the relationships of your contacts — putting in Joe Doakes' record that you were referred to him by Mary Smith, for example.

We'd like you to slightly change your thinking about your contacts and how you manage them.

Don't fit the people you connect with on social media into your standard contact management system. Of course, you need to database the basic information; we're not saying you don't need their digits.

But rather than thinking about a contact list, a Rolodex, or any other kind of static list of people you know, think instead about the web of relationships that the people you know represents. Joe knows Mary who knows Sandy who knows Stan who needs what you're selling. That's true, but that's linear thinking.

In reality Joe not only knows Mary, but also Phil and Dave and Bill and Jen, and maybe Sandy and Stan, and each of them in turn know dozens or hundreds of others. Somewhere in that web of community are people who are ready to buy what you're selling. Who you know is not some hierarchical, static list of phone numbers to dial. Rather, these people are constantly changing, evolving into new jobs, creating their own new relationships.

Add to this complex network the fact that the people in your organization have similar communities that not only intersect with yours, but may represent stronger connections to prospects. Given all this, we hope you can see that viewing sales as an exercise in powering through enough sales calls to turn up a sale is limiting.

Whether or not you create a formal Infinite Pipeline community, you can approach the sea of people you know in a way that maximizes relationship-building.

Rather than only evaluating your network by who you know, try to realize the value of what you know about who you know.

A quick, pre-Internet example: A sales guy we know had been trying to get into an organization for some time without results. Carl was selling motivational gifts, and he knew he had to talk to the CEO to get anywhere. Every week he showed up in the CEO's office, to the point that he got to know the administrative assistant, DeeDee, very well. She confided to Carl that the CEO would never agree to see him. Through his conversations with DeeDee, Carl learned that the CEO was a big model train fan.

Stymied by the conventional approach, Carl went out and bought a very expensive train set with an engine, a caboose, and several cars. He dropped the caboose into a box and sent it anonymously to the CEO. The next week, he sent another car, and then another and another until only the engine was left. He then showed up in the CEO's office with a box under his arm. "Is he in, DeeDee?" he asked. "You know he won't see you," she said. "Give him this," Carl replied. "But don't tell him I gave it to you." DeeDee gave Carl a quizzical look, but brought the box into the CEO's office. A minute later, the CEO rushed out into the foyer to see who had been sending him the train cars.

"Oh," he exclaimed. "Dammit, Carl. It's you. Well, you might as well come in, but I can tell you, I'm not buying." That day Carl convinced the CEO to take a chance on one little piece of business with him and eventually he had the whole account.

So, did smiling and dialing work for this account? Nope. Did the fact that Carl was on a first name basis with the decision-maker close the sale? No. But what Carl knew about his prospect did.

What do you know about your prospects? If they're on social media, you will be surprised how much more you can find out. Not only does social media provide you the access to these hard-to-get prospects — through LinkedIn Groups, or Facebook, or Twitter — it provides the means to get to know them better, and to create and develop a relationship.

Here's what you should do before calling on a new contact or organization:

- Research the company Website (especially press releases or blogs)

- Search for LinkedIn profiles on Google

- Search LinkedIn for:

  » Profiles of key executives

  » The groups your targets belong to, especially groups you also belong to

  » Accomplishments or anything especially important to your targets

- Search for other individuals or organizations in the industry to identify news, common challenges, and so on

  » Political or regulatory changes

  » New technologies

  » Changes similar organizations are making

Using this information, broaden the profiles you have of your prospects and begin to hone in on top targets. Once you've got a list, use the following Infinite Pipeline Relationship Development Process that got Robbie past the gatekeepers at the multinational and which we detail later in this chapter on page 166.

Map the Relationships

Many current CRM systems aren't flexible enough to really map the web of interconnections that already exist in the real world, but which become even more important when you try to organize the social media world.

It's not enough to just track who referred you, or how you know a certain contact. You need to track not only who you know, but what you know about them and also what you know about who they know, and on and on.

One good system that we've seen is Jason Alba's JibberJobber.[96] It helps you track the interrelationships of the people you know. Another is InsideView,[97] which has a free option to get you started. Salesforce.com[98] now enables social media profiles and internal social media features as part of its CRM product. You can even use a product such PersonalBrain[99] to really visualize the cloud of people you know and how they're connected.

Undoubtedly, the current CRM systems will evolve even further to provide you the means to track what Facebook calls the Social Graph. The Social Graph depicts personal relationships and maps everybody on Facebook, and cooperating sites, and how they're related. If you've ever visited a site, and they ask you if you'd like to use Facebook to log in, that site is using Facebook's Social Graph facility. This obviously gives Facebook and participating sites a lot of information about how people are related. Imagine if your CRM could show you a map of all your relationships? It would likely be much less complex than this visualization of Facebook's global Social Graph:

---

96 JibberJobber: bit.ly/Nt81rG
97 InsideView: bit.ly/Mq8yYm
98 Salesforce.com's The Social Enterprise Solution: bit.ly/LOrpAd
99 TheBrain Technologies' PersonalBrain: bit.ly/NknNAZ

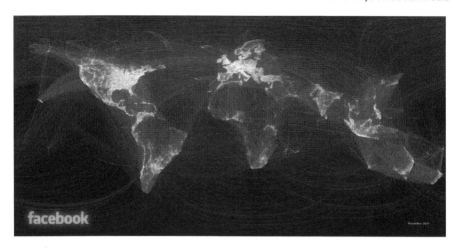

Figure 32 - Facebook's Global Social Graph Visualization[100]

In your current relationship tracking, chances are you're focusing mainly on tracking decision-makers: people in the C-Suite, director-level folks and such. However, you probably know that influencers — those who can affect a decision or deliver a lead, but who lack a fancy title — can also be very important to the sales process.

There's a whole discipline around network analysis, which attempts to determine who the influencers are in an organization, often by analyzing various internal communications. One classic example of the result of network analysis is the recent finding that if you are obese, your friends are more likely to be obese, and their friends, and so on.[101]

Other types of behavior spread this way, including sales decisions. Robbie landed the multinational whose procurement guy who laughed at him by networking for nine months with a low-level project manager, not with VPs or directors or other decision-makers. Her recommendation that Robbie's company be allowed to bid on the business was the key to that sale. She wasn't the only lower-level employee that Robbie networked with. He targeted a dozen or so. But, as they say, all it takes is one.

So when you use social networking for prospecting, don't forget the "little people." Good sales people already know this, and cultivate in particular the various gatekeeper admins, assistants, and others who surround the decision-makers. But other influencers outside the company can be equally crucial. Our

100 Mashable's *The World's Facebook Relationships Visualized*: on.mash.to/Nt6PV2
101 The Sociograph's *Is obesity contagious? A Review of the Debate over the "Network Effects" of Obesity*: bit.ly/L0XYqF

company received a great entree into a large pharmaceutical company because while catching a plane, one of our members ran into a childhood friend who works for them.

You've probably gotten leads like that in your career. Using social media, you can follow similar leads by analyzing your contacts' interests, clubs, and group and association memberships.

A great way to start finding connections is using LinkedIn profiles. When you connect with someone, you can see their connections unless they've prevented it with a profile setting. LinkedIn helps find the connections you have in common by listing them when you visit a profile. If you visit the profile of a connection's connection (your second level network) you can see the connections and groups you have in common.

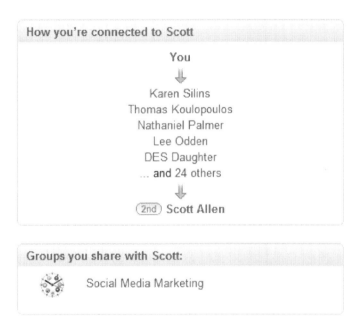

Figure 33 - LinkedIn Shows How You Can Connect to a Second Level Connection

If you visit the profile of a third level connection, LinkedIn also shows how you can connect.

now you re connected to Spencer

You
⇓
George McGowan III
Mike O'Neil
Matt Zaske
Matthew Rochte
Barb Zilmer
... and 21 others
⇓
Spencer's connections
⇓
(3rd) Spencer M.

Figure 34 – LinkedIn Doesn't Show Second Level Connections to Third Level Targets

LinkedIn doesn't show you the second level connections that would enable you to connect with third level target contacts because they want you to get your first level connections to introduce you.

Nevertheless, gathering information about who in your first level can get you connected is valuable.

Even if you don't try to connect with second or third level contacts right away, add the significant ones to your network map. Try to map out all your important social media connections on all your social media sites in this manner.

Identify Prospects Who Use LinkedIn Often

To figure out which of your prospects to target on LinkedIn, your first step should be to determine how often they use LinkedIn. Many executives on LinkedIn rarely use it and so an indirect approach may work better.

Visit the prospect's profile and take a look at their activity stream and their current status. If you don't see much activity, you may want to use LinkedIn to find influencers rather than approaching the prospect directly on LinkedIn.

If the prospect is an active LinkedIn user, note that in your network map. Obviously, if a prospect uses LinkedIn a lot, it's much easier to begin your relationship with them on the site.

Make a list of heavy LinkedIn users and be sure to visit their profiles on a regular basis to see what they're up to. Comment or Like their status updates as the first step in building a relationship with them.

Understand LinkedIn InMails

InMail is an internal LinkedIn messaging system that enables you to send a message to anyone on LinkedIn, regardless of whether you are connected to them. Although InMails can be a good way to connect with a prospect, you should use them sparingly because, frankly, they're just another kind of cold call.

If the InMail is unwanted, not relevant, or otherwise annoying, not only can it turn off the prospect, but they can report you to LinkedIn.

The LinkedIn free account lets you pay to send InMails, although from time to time LinkedIn will run a promotion letting you send an InMail for free. To get free InMails, you need to upgrade to a paid account.

- **Business Account** — 3 InMails/month

- **Business Plus Account** — 10 InMails/month

- **Pro Account** (AKA Executive Account) — 25 InMails/month

At some levels (recruiter accounts, for example) you can get unlimited InMails.

Judicious use of this capability can help you in your prospecting, but it's always a good idea to follow our messaging guidelines from the section *Get Your Messaging Straight* on page 112 when crafting your messages. This means offer a good reason for contacting the prospect, and don't do any hard selling.

Mike has noticed a trend of people out of his network sending rank advertising and marketing messages via InMails recently. So far the number is manageable so he sends back a note asking the person to stop sending the messages, but at some point, it just becomes easier to report abuse to LinkedIn, which could result in suspension for the sender.

Nobody likes spam, so be careful with this powerful tool.

Start Connecting in the Real World

Once you've advanced your relationship with a prospect to an appropriate point — generally after exchanging several online messages — it may be time to ask for a meeting.

We're not going to pretend to know the best way for you to do this, but we'll give some general guidelines.

It's probably best to start with a low-risk invitation to meet for coffee or to chat while you're both at some event. We probably would not start with an invitation to your company's event, or to come in for a pitch meeting. You're still getting to know the person.

Similarly, try to make the purpose of the meeting all about the prospect and their interests. Saying, "I'd like to hear more about that problem you were describing to me the other day" or "I'd like to hear your views on [industry trend]" is much better than a generic "I'd like to get to know you better."

From here on, it's mostly Sales 101, except remember: don't pitch. Follow our Infinite Pipeline Relationship Development Process, which we describe in detail in the next section.

Infinite Pipeline Relationship Development Process

Here's the technique that Robbie has used to close millions of dollars of business. It's simple, easy, but effective. And it doesn't require any sales pitches. The goal is to develop a community that will sell for you by creating and growing relationships.

- Find people in target organizations

- Look them up on LinkedIn

- Join the groups they are in

- See if they've posted in the group discussions and then comment

- Try to engage them in a conversation on the group forum

- When the time is right, suggest that you connect on LinkedIn

- Once you are connected download their vCard, which usually contains their email address

- Email them periodically (don't spam) with a bit of news or other information that they will be interested in, and ask for their comments

- Watch their activity and comment as appropriate

- When the time is right, ask to have coffee — concentrate the conversation on them. Don't pitch.

- Repeat. Continue to offer solutions.

What? No close?

That's right, no close. During the process, your contact will ask you about your business. Keep your responses short, personal, sales-free, and focused on activities that are relevant to your contact's business problems. For example, you might say, "Well, I'm a little concerned about making my son's soccer game next week because we've got a big sales training session scheduled about the new product release."

If your contact wants more details — and asks specifically for them — feel free to discuss. But no pitch, no close.

What you'll find is that your prospect will ask you for the sales meeting or product details. During this phase, use one of Robbie's favorite phrases: "I don't even know if this is going to be a fit for you, but let's take a look."

Not only does this create an environment in which you and the prospect can explore the solution, it tends to put a lot of the sales responsibility on the buyer. The more time they invest, the more they're going to want to prove that your product is a fit. In other words, they can sell themselves. Without a close.

You may not think that this could work, but it does, and Robbie has the commissions to prove it.

Use Automated Tools

So far, most of your effort – and the advice in this book – has emphasized manual processes. You need to remember to check your LinkedIn activity stream, to check your prospects' statuses, to follow LinkedIn Group discussions, and so on.

Luckily, there are some good, free tools that will enable you to become aware of important changes in your prospects' lives automatically.

By the same token, there are free tools that let you automate your contributions on social networking sites. We take a brief look at notification tools and automated posting tools in the following sections.

Notification Tools

These tools can help you keep abreast of news and changes from your social media contacts by sending you an email when certain information about your prospects changes.

Job Change Notifier

LinkedIn will notify you in your activity stream when a contact changes jobs, but it's easy to miss if you don't keep close tabs. Job Change Notifier[102] is a simple free application that will let you know about job changes via email.

Rapportive for Gmail

Rapportive is a plug-in for Google Gmail that brings up a sidebar whenever you open or compose an email. Rapportive reads the email address of the sender or recipient and posts in the sidebar relevant information from the person's social media.

Information usually includes the person's picture, their LinkedIn or Twitter bio, and their various social media accounts, with links and recent posts. If the person is in your address book, Rapportive also displays their contact info and any recent emails.

This is a great way to keep apprised of what your contacts are doing, and quickly and easily go to the relevant social media site and comment.

Outlook Social Connector and Xobni

Microsoft's Outlook Social Connector[103] enables you to synchronize your contacts' social media data right into Outlook. You can also see status updates from various social networks without leaving Outlook.

Xobni[104] also integrates into Outlook and does much the same thing, as well as consolidating all of your various address books from your phone, Gmail, and Outlook and other programs.

Automated Posting Tools

These tools allow you to post the same material to several different social media sites as well as to schedule multiple posts so they are spread out throughout the day or are posted at a future date and time. They also help you organize and filter your social media feeds in a single interface for easy reading.

---

102 Job Change Notifier: bit.ly/MddumR
103 Microsoft Outlook Social Connector: bit.ly/Nt976G
104 Xobni: bit.ly/KSkWEW

HootSuite

HootSuite is a great automation tool and one of the most full-featured available. The free version is quite powerful, and the paid version offers even more features.

HootSuite enables you to:

Schedule updates on multiple supported social networks

- Produce robust statistics on how your posts perform
- Manage multiple accounts using multiple users
- Create public and private lists of connections
- Save posts as templates to repeat postings
- Upload videos and photos and measure their results
- Import Twitter lists and watch them in separate columns
- Search networks in real time

Tweetdeck

Tweetdeck is now part of Twitter and it offers a lot of functionality to help you make sense of your social media feeds. Tweetdeck enables you to follow feeds from multiple sites by assigning each to a column in the software. You can also add columns that follow particular people, keywords, or which filter out people you don't want to see.

There are a variety of competitors to Tweetdeck including Seesmic, Echofon, Sobees, and Alternion. You may want to check them out before deciding which to use. However, if you're serious about following Twitter feeds, you might want to choose Tweetdeck as Twitter is likely to start integrating the tool into the way it organizes feeds.

Buffer

Buffer is a tool that lets you schedule LinkedIn, Facebook, Twitter, and blog updates. Once installed, it shows up as an option when you create a Facebook or Twitter post. Submitting the post to Buffer schedules the post according to parameters you've set up on the Buffer Website. For example, you can spread your posts out every hour, or post only at certain times of the day.

The free version will queue up only 10 posts at a time, and will spread them over multiple days if you desire.

There are other free post-scheduling tools, including the aforementioned HootSuite, Timely (which queues unlimited posts), and Crowdbooster. If the free versions don't provide the capacity you need, you can use multiple tools to schedule your posts the way you want or you can pay for premium versions.

Create Your Own Communities

Many of the techniques involved in the Infinite Pipeline sales development system require buy-in and action from other members of your organization, most notably sales management. But creating your own personal Infinite Pipeline community is completely within your control. And the key to doing this is to create a place online for your community to assemble where you can nurture your interrelationships.

There are two main ways to do this without involving a lot of other people in your organization: creating a LinkedIn Group and starting a blog.

You should consider doing both these things but be prepared: You can't set it and forget it. Take some of your prospect development time and devote it to the care and feeding of the communities you create around your LinkedIn Group and/or your blog.

Both are very easy to set up, and we detail processes and strategy in the next two sections.

Create a LinkedIn Group

One great way to build your brand and extend your prospecting on LinkedIn is to create your own group. We don't recommend naming the group after your company unless you want to have a group for current or former staff. Rather, determine a concept or problem of concern to your target audience and create a group around that.

You should name the group using keywords, because it's all about search, especially since there are more 1.3 million groups on LinkedIn, with the largest representing more than 200,000 members.

But don't create a group without a plan. By creating a group, you are making a commitment to your community, and you had better figure out what you're going to do before you take the plunge.[105]

---

105 LinkedIn guide on creating a group: bit.ly/mmQtVz

LinkedIn Group Strategy

There are two general types of groups on LinkedIn: open groups and closed groups. The choices are known as "Open Access" and "Request to Join" on the group creation form. More specifically, you can designate your group as:

• Alumni	• Corporate
• Conference	• Networking
• Non-Profit	• Professional
• Other	

You'll be able to upload a logo for the group, so you should think about whether you need a new logo or if you'll use your company's logo.

Group search is only done on the 300-word group summary so make sure it contains keywords that potential members are likely to use to find the group. Other important settings are:

- **Display this group in the Group directory** — If you want to be found, be sure to check this.

- **Allow group members to display the logo on their profiles** — This is another great way to get found; often members will check out the groups their connections belong to. It's a good idea to post a message on the group's discussion forum encouraging members to display the group logo on their profiles.

- **Pre-approve members with the following email domain(s)** — This is especially useful for alumni and corporate groups

Once you've created the group, you can explicitly invite 200 of your contacts to join. Be sure to do that.

Next, you'll need a plan to recruit members. Decide what kinds of people you'd like to join, and target them on LinkedIn using the techniques described in the earlier sections.

You also need to establish a policy on the types of posts that will be permitted on the group. As group manager, you have plenty of power to police the group, but you need to be sure group members understand your policies.

Among the policies you'll need to consider:

- **Vulgar, profane or other negative messages** — Make your policy clear on these points, and the fact that you can expel members who violate group policies

- **Preventing LION Invites** — LIONs love groups and often repeatedly cross-post invitations for members to connect with them. You need to decide whether to prohibit this type of posting, and how you'll deal with LIONs in general.

- **Prevent Members from Repeatedly Posting the Same Post** — You'll find that some of your members will view the group solely as a way to promote themselves or their event. Establish a policy regarding this and other repetitive posts.

Finally, even if you're not too interested in creating a group, depending on your situation you may want to do so anyway, just to preempt someone else from doing it. For example, the ex-Microsoft employee LinkedIn group is run by an Apple recruiter. Think seriously about this if your business has a vocal opposition that might want to create a group under your name just to trash you.

Create a Blog

It's very easy, and free, to start a blog. It's harder to create a blog that will amass a following, or make a difference. Like all the social media sites we discuss in this book, you should start with a plan that includes your goals, the audience you are trying to reach, the tone of the blog, the name and branding of the blog, your marketing plan, and a publishing schedule. You may want to get your friends in marketing involved as well.

There are all kinds of free blog platforms available that will host your blog. The most popular are Wordpress, Typepad, Blogsmith, Blogger, and Movable Type. Here's a short list of sites to consider:[106]

- Wordpress.com

- Blogger.com

- Blogspot.com

- LiveJournal.com

---

106 There's a good overview of blogging platforms and a list of the top 100 blogs and their blogging platforms at: bit.ly/9ooHQO

How to Blog

There are as many ways to blog as there are people on Earth. Each blogger will approach the task of posting an engaging blog in his or her own way. As we indicated above, you should decide how blogging will achieve your online objectives before you start.

Start by Commenting

Once you've created your plan and figured out your approach, visit lots of relevant blogs and consider posting comments as a way to get the hang of blogging. In doing so, keep in mind the following guidelines for commenting on others' posts:

- **Follow the 4-to-1 rule**: Comment on four posts for every post that you write — Spread the love around

- **Follow the 4-1-1 rule**: This rule for Twitter is a good rule for all social media: For every one self-serving post, you should repost one relevant post from another blog and most importantly, share four pieces of relevant content written by others.[107]

- **Comments are a great way to spread the word, but don't spam** — If every comment you make includes a gratuitous link to your blog, or is seen as merely self-serving, you're not going to be successful in luring readers of other blogs to yours

- **Ensure your comments are relevant and on-topic** — This is the other side of the previous rule: Don't comment if you're not adding value. We're often tempted to post something useless like "I agree," or "What he said" but that does nothing but clutter up the comments stream, and readers will immediately gloss over your comment in search of something interesting.

- **Always acknowledge a repost** — If another blogger links to you, quotes you, or reposts you, be sure to visit their blog and at least post a thank you comment

- **Link to other blogs** — Acknowledging a great post on another's blog can help build your reputation and deliver readers for your own blog

- **Include a link to your blog** — Yes, it's appropriate to include a link to your blog in a comment, but only in context, meaning that your blog amplifies or otherwise is pertinent to the same or a similar topic

---

107   Marketo's *The 4-1-1 Rule for Lead Nurturing*: bit.ly/PvTuKC

Blog Regularly

Once you start blogging, you'll want to establish a rhythm. Try to blog frequently — more than once a week, maybe even daily. The point of you blogging is to get followers. Followers want currency, not stale, month-old posts. Blogging frequently will keep them coming back.

If you can't commit to blog daily, shoot for blogging every few days, or at least weekly. You may need to spread the blogging chores among several authors. If you do, encourage them to maintain a common tone. It's important to blog regularly, meaning according to a schedule. If you blog once a week, for example, pick a day so your followers know when to expect your posts.

Writing Your Blog

One of the most important things to keep in mind when writing a blog is: You have seconds to capture the reader, and it's very easy to lose them after the first paragraph.

Create a Great Title

Your blog needs a great title, and so do your blog posts. Whether it's short and to the point, or long and quirky, your title has to grab the reader. Research shows that people's decision to read an article is heavily dependent on the title of the article.[108]

If you've read a newspaper or magazine lately (work with us here, GenY), you're familiar with the concept. Chances are good you thumb through the periodical scanning the titles and headlines (and pictures — we'll get to them later) until something looks good. Then you read the first paragraph and decide if you want to read more. If the article isn't delivering what you want, you move on.

On the Web this process is multiplied a thousand-fold. If you're lucky enough for your blog post to make it onto the front page of Google, its title must jump out as the prospective reader rapidly scans the search results. Remember: On the Web, every click is a commitment. You're leaving the familiar comfort of the page you're on to venture into the unknown in the optimistic hope of finding something useful, entertaining, or informative. And if the article doesn't deliver on the promise of the title, your reader is off to the next adventure.

---

108 Jack B. Haskins' paper *Title-Rating: A Method for Measuring Reading Interests and Predicting Readership*: bit.ly/cfGcZl

Create a Great Lead

Blog posts must get right to the point. Study some of the most influential blogs, such as the Huffington Post[109] or Gawker.[110] Watch how they hook the reader in. Here's an example of a HuffPost article lead:

> For all his retro failings and inability to open up, Don Draper has always been intrigued, even turned on, by women who are willing to stand up to him and are smart enough to argue with him.

Who's that lead targeted to? Yup. Women.

How about this lead from Gawker:

> There's a melodramatic "war" brewing between Facebook and Google, and Facebook's CEO is seizing the opportunity to squeeze more work from his engineers, declaring a "lockdown," keeping the office open on weekends, and putting a neon sign on his door.

Target audience? People like you, who read books about social computing!

Write and rewrite your lead so that it communicates the promise of the post and entices the reader to continue.

Add Pictures

Remember when you were thumbing through the magazine in your imagination in the previous section? You were scanning titles, but you were also looking at the pictures. Since many of your audience members will belong to the post-literate generations, consider including at least one grabber of a picture in each blog post.

Try to make the picture caption tell a mini-story within the story. This helps with search engine optimization

Use Pull Quotes

Also known as a lift-out quote or a call-out, a pull quote is a quotation or edited excerpt from a post placed in a larger typeface and embedded in a text box to entice readers and to highlight a key topic. You've probably seen them on the

This is a pull quote!
Notice how it grabs attention.

---

109 Huffington Post: huff.to/9bAbxA
110 Gawker: bit.ly/9czGyt

professional news sites and blogs. It's a great way to provide more cues to your readers about what your post is about.

Write Scannable Text

Since your prospective readers are going to quickly scan your article to decide on its relevance, be sure to write in a way that enables scanning. This means no long, laborious, clause-laden sentences. Write in a shorter, choppier style that quickly imparts the information. And use lots of white space, especially between paragraphs.

Use bulleted lists. You may have noticed we have a lot of them in this book. Take a moment and scan back 30 or 40 pages. See how the bulleted lists attract your eye, and quickly give you a sense of what's on the page, and what the topic under discussion is?

Notice that we use a lot of white space as well, often setting sentences off apart from the rest of the text.

That's not the way you were taught to write in school, but that's what works in the increasingly attention-deficit world we're living in.

So keep your paragraphs short, and don't be afraid to make them only a sentence long.

Keep it Short

Pundits differ on the precise recommended post length, but pretty much everyone agrees blog posts should be short. We think you should aim for 300-500 words. As a guide, the average 8 ½" x 11" page has roughly 400 words on it.

If your topic is long and involved, split your post into multiple pages of about 500 words each. If your topic really demands more extensive coverage, consider making it into a series of posts. Mike did this when a blog site asked him to do a guest post on business use of LinkedIn. They suggested 500-700 words for the whole article. Mike replied that there was no way to do the topic justice in that amount, and ended up doing a five-part series.

You'll need to figure out the length issue yourself. We suggest you ask your community what they think. Perhaps you always leave them wanting more. Perhaps they get tired of reading you after half a page. Remember that it doesn't matter what you think when it comes to these issues. It's what your audience thinks. And the great thing is: You can ask them.

Good Blog Topics

Once you start blogging, one of your first concerns is going to be, "What do I blog about?"

Chances are you have plenty of possible topics. But what's going to connect with your community? Probably not updates on your latest product release. Probably not your company's latest award. Once again, you'll have to figure this out for yourself, but here's a list of suggestions that may work.

- **Create Top N Lists** — Creating blog posts that offer top 10 (or whatever number) lists is a proven winner. It promises a quick, easily-digestible take on a subject. Google the phrase "Top 10"[111] and see 650 million great examples.

- **Top People/Products** — A variation of top n lists that adds the promise of celebrity

- **Be Contrarian** — Disagreeing with established opinion can be a draw. People often seek this type of alternative to accepted wisdom.

- **Be Controversial** — But not too controversial. You're looking to stir up debate, not trouble.

- **Answer FAQs** — FAQs are Frequently Asked Questions. Every field has them. If you promise to answer them, people will be likely to read.

- **Exhibit Thought Leadership** — Find an issue that is debated within your industry, and simply state your position on it. Study it, consider it, form an opinion, and then write a post laying your opinion and justifying it.

- **Ask Questions** — Asking people about their favorites is a popular method: "What's your favorite movie?"

Maintaining Your Community

As we've said, you can create an Infinite Pipeline community by yourself, using social media. The trick is to create one that is sustainable. That means you can't be the only voice in the community. If you spend a lot of time asking people what they think and engaging in back and forth commenting, you're much more likely to sustain your community. And if you keep the salesiness to a minimum, that will help your success as well. Many people will join your community because they are interested in what you're selling. Your task is to figure out the balance between to much product information and pitches and too little.

---

111 Made you look! Here's the Top 10 Google search for your convenience: bit.ly/O3GSN5

If you're interested in learning more about this, or any of the concepts in this book, there are three things you can do:

- Get our other book, *The Infinite Pipeline: How to Master Social Media for Business-to-Business Sales Success, Sales Executive Edition.* That book contains a lot more practical advice about building and maintaining communities.

- Get our book, *Be a Person - The Social Operating Manual for Enterprises,*[112] a 400+ page step-by-step manual that contains everything you need to build your social presence online — Fast!

- Contact us about our sales training programs through our Website, **socialmediaperformancegroup.com.**

---

112 Social Media Performance Group's *Be a Person - The Social Operating Manual for Enterprises*: *bit.ly/OrderBeAPerson*

Afterword

Today, more B2B companies than ever are discovering the potential of branded online communities – but be careful – branding should always take a backseat.

Forrester Research
Deepen B2B Tech Customer Engagement
With Community Marketing

Well, that's it. A quick overview of everything you need to build your Infinite Pipeline and supercharge your sales.

Because social media is so fast-moving, lots of the details in this book will rapidly become obsolete, perhaps by the time you read this. But the overarching Infinite Pipeline concepts, we feel, will survive the constantly-changing details. The sites may change; new capabilities may emerge; and certainly some new bright shiny thing will unseat the current 400-pound social media gorillas.

But sales doesn't change — basically — over the eons. People always feel better buying from friends and close acquaintances. Nobody likes to be sold, but everyone likes to buy. The social media techniques in this book are complements to the basic knowledge and techniques that all good salespeople have.

We hope we've made some sense of this onrushing phenomenon, and we flatter ourselves to hope the advice in this book will remain relevant no matter how social computing evolves.

We'd like to hear from you, not only about what you think of our advice, but what you learn as you create your own social media practice. You can contribute by commenting on the Social Media Performance Group's Website at

www.SocialMediaPerformanceGroup.com

Be careful out there and remember, Don't Panic!

Who is the
Social Media Performance Group?

Social Media Performance Group is a premier enterprise social media consulting company that offers a unique approach to integrating social media into the enterprise — forget about the tools, it's all about the strategy!

Rather than focusing on the tactics (do this or that on LinkedIn, Twitter, YouTube), first we work with you and your senior leadership to comprehend your corporate strategy. Once we understand your strategic objectives and goals, we show you how a comprehensive social media strategy can integrate with and support your corporate strategy.

We take an enterprise-wide view based on our unique Enterprise Social Media Framework, which maps social media to all appropriate touchpoints in your enterprise. We go beyond the obvious quick hits and help you achieve social-media-driven results in areas such as product development, customer service, and employee engagement and retention.

As a result, social media is not just bolted on; it is integrated with, and provides support for, your company's existing strategy and operations, yielding unprecedented results.

 The three principals of SMPG have varied and complementary capabilities and experience. We also partner with world class marketing, branding, design, and development resources to offer complete strategy-to-execution services.

We invite you to:

- Like our Facebook page at: www.facebook.com/SocialMediaPerformance

- Check out our Webpage at: socialmediaperformancegroup.com

- Join our community at community.socialmediaperformancegroup.com

- Follow our blog at: smperformance.wordpress.com

Mike Ellsworth

Mike has been buying enterprise technology solutions for more than 20 years and has met, worked with, and been (sometimes) annoyed by every kind of B2B sales person. He even briefly sold vacuum cleaners a long time ago while in graduate school, and experience which firmly convinced him that he's not a sales guy.

Mike's background includes experience as an IT Program Manager, Chief Technology Officer, Vice President of Strategic Planning, Senior Project Manager, and as an independent Emerging Technology Strategy Consultant.

Most recently he leveraged more than a decade of social media experience (his first social media proposal was in 2001) by starting Linked InSolutions, a social media training and consulting company and subsequently helping found Social Media Performance Group.

During his 15-year career at the Nielsen Company in the marketing research business, he helped set Dun & Bradstreet's Internet strategy and developed the vision that resulted in the consumer packaged goods industry's first Web application in early 1995. With his company, StratVantage Consulting, Mike helped Sterling Commerce create their ecommerce strategy and has helped senior leaders understand and connect rapidly changing new technologies with the organization's existing strategy.

An award-winning writer with an extensive background in technical and creative writing, Mike is the principal author of Social Media Performance Group's **Be a Person** and Infinite Pipeline series of books as well as the Social Media Performance Group blog (smperformance.wordpress.com).

Mike holds a BA in Psychology from Duke University and did post-graduate work in writing at the University of Denver and the Naropa Institute.

Mike tweets at **@MikeEllsworth.**

Ken Morris, JD

In addition to being a founding principal of SMPG, Ken is President and CEO of Aperçu Group Inc., a team of leading scholars and practitioners dedicated to helping organizations improve their financial and operational performance, and co-founder, President and CEO of CorCardia Group, Inc., a global medical supply chain firm that develops leading-edge inventory management solutions for medical device companies and hospitals.

In addition to social media consulting, Ken consults and coaches on issues of diversity, leadership, conflict management, succession planning, crisis management, team building, negotiation, presentation skills, workplace systems design, marketing, and strategic planning.

Ken's accomplishments include helping improve his customers' financial and operational performance; ecommerce and technology integration; Internet, intranet, networking and information technology; recruitment and retention; business and human resources strategy and execution; marketing and business development; international affairs; executive development, education and training; and community and governmental affairs.

Ken is a former Vice President of Human Resources at Boston Scientific and Guidant, Vice President, Business Development at Professional Development Group, Inc., and previously held positions at Honeywell and State Farm.

Ken holds a J.D. from Hamline University School of Law and a BmED in Music from Willamette University.

Ken tweets at **@smpgcom.**

Robbie Johnson

The third founding principal of SMPG, Robbie is an experienced business development and channel sales manager who is adept at effectively creating a community of customers and prospects to attract new business, close sales, and increase company revenue. He has successfully worked with a wide array of organizations ranging from Fortune 100 companies to small, local companies to non-profits and charity organizations.

Robbie has a history of using new approaches to adapt sales processes and the relationship sell to the constantly evolving business-to-business environment to successfully close millions of dollars of sales and partnerships. Over the past five years, Robbie has focused on pioneering the use of social media in three different B2B environments: one of the world's largest software companies, a small IT consulting firm, and as channel manager of a medium-sized software-as-service (SaaS) company.

Along the way he has mentored dozens of his colleagues in using social media to connect with friends and coworkers and developed the concepts that lead to the creation of the Infinite Pipeline sales development system. He's used these techniques effectively to land new clients and prospects, including some of the largest companies in the world.

For Robbie, social selling isn't the latest bright shiny thing, full of unproven, half-baked concepts and theories. Social selling is based on proven, sustainable, real-world techniques that result in sales, commissions, and partnerships.

Robbie holds a BS in Industrial Psychology from Metropolitan State University.

Robbie tweets at **@rjohnsoninc.**

Acknowledgements

The editing and finishing of this book was an exercise in crowdsourcing. We are grateful for the assistance of the following reviewers, many of whom responded to our LinkedIn Question, who substantially improved this book:

Reviewer	Description
Michelle Tresemer	Michelle has been involved in social media for more than 10 years and works with small business and nonprofit clients to develop strategic marketing plans including social media strategy. This includes creating branded Facebook pages, custom applications, and training organizations how to use data to increase donations, engagement, sales, or awareness. She earned her MBA in Nonprofit Management from Marylhurst University and a BA in Advertising from Pepperdine University.
Camille Rodriquez	Camille Rodriquez is an author, business owner, and "Social Media Impressionist." She founded Polka Dot Impressions, a social media marketing and management company, and she has written extensively on the subject of social media. She has also published a book entitled, "When I Die: On Being, Living, and Having the Last Word," in which she talks about living an intentional, purposeful life!

Reviewer	Description
Charlene Burke	Charlene Burke is CEO of Search by Burke, LLC, a full service online marketing agency that focuses on helping their clients create, develop and maintain their online presence to increase sales. Charlene acknowledges that her skills in traditional sales techniques are nominal. Instead, she uses various social media platforms to connect with professionals, learn about industries and companies, ask questions of prospects before they know they're prospects, then takes the relationship offline so it can flourish as a long term client relationship.
Julio Viskovich	Julio has worked with a number of Fortune 500 companies including InBev, Roger's Wireless, and Microsoft to develop, implement, and deliver national sales training and social media education programs. Julio currently heads enterprise inside sales training at Canada's tech darling HootSuite. To connect with Julio visit him at **http://www.JulioViskovich.com**.

Reviewer	Description
David Howard	David is an internet marketing consultant working in the San Francisco Bay Area. David has twenty years of progressive experience in customer support, product management and online marketing spanning telecommunications, Internet applications and cloud-computing software. He has worked with NASDAQ 100 firms and early-stage startups alike.

Reviewer	Description
Sam Richter	Sam Richter is an internationally recognized expert on sales and marketing. His experience includes building innovative and award-winning technology, sales, and marketing programs for start-up companies and some of the world's most famous brands. Sam was named one of the Most Influential Chief Marketing Officers on Twitter, and one of the nation's Top 25 Most Influential Sales Leaders. He is a member of the Business Journal's Forty Under 40, and he is a past finalist for Inc. Magazine's Entrepreneur of the Year. Sam is SVP/CMO at ActiFi, one of the financial industry's foremost practice management coaching and software firms. His most recent best-selling book, Take the Cold Out of Cold Calling is now in multiple editions and has also won numerous awards including 2012 Sales Book of the Year, as selected by the 1,500 member companies of the AA-ISP. Through his top-rated Know More! programs, Sam has trained teams and entertained tens of thousands of persons around the world. Learn what others say about Sam's programs at www.samrichter.com/reviews

Reviewer	Description
Jill Konrath	Jill is the author of two bestselling sales books and is a popular speaker who helps sellers crack into new accounts, speed up sales cycles and win more business. *SNAP Selling*, her highly acclaimed new book, jumped to #1 on Amazon within hours of its release — and continues to be a top seller. Jill's first book, *Selling to Big Companies*, addressed a major sales problem that continues today: how to set up meetings with prospects who'd rather avoid salespeople all together. Fortune named it one of eight "must reads" for sellers, along with *How to Win Friends & Influence People, The New Strategic Selling* and *Getting to Yes*. It's also been an Amazon Top 25 sales book since 2006.

Reviewer	Description
Chris Cortilet	Chris is Creative Director at Pilcrow Partners, LLC. He has 25 years experience developing strategies for brands in traditional and digital marketing. His breadth and depth of business and marketing experience helps Chris look into any problem-solving situation with confidence. Chris works with organizations to see their brand through the lens of their business goals. It's important to create a consistent vision when in today's market the complexity of new and dynamic marketing paradigms can become a distraction. Chris evaluates company goals and then aligns them with effective marketing strategies, often finding new valued revenue streams that cut cost, create operational efficiency or engage your customers in new and compelling ways.

Sales Communities

Here are some existing sales communities.

Community	Link
HME Sales Community	**bit.ly/ImsdZ4**
American Express' Business Travel ConneXion	**bit.ly/MzQprc**
SPS Commerce's Retail Universe	**bit.ly/KCo1D5**
The Wholesale Forums	**bit.ly/OpKklw**
Cisco - Social@Cisco	**bit.ly/LAn4wS**
SAP - SAP Community Network	**bit.ly/MZh9Sa**
Intel - Intel Software Network Communities	**intel.ly/NE2g5Y**
IBM	**ibm.co/NJOh3p**
Siemens	**bit.ly/VAPFqB**
Kinaxis	**bit.ly/PTehfK**
GE - MarkNet	**bit.ly/PTdJ9x** (article)
EMC - RSA Archer Community	**bit.ly/MnfR1u**
Cree - CreeLEDrevolution	**bit.ly/LcwQ6S**
RICS - MyRics	**bit.ly/Lcxd17**
RS Components - Design Spark	**bit.ly/SdilVp**

ShipServ	**bit.ly/NPHcMl**
UPS - "We ♥ Logistics"	**bit.ly/P3dWEH**
Bank of America - Small Business Community	**bit.ly/P3e4nr**
Kodak - Grow Your Biz	**bit.ly/Nkp5Ag**

Everything you need to build your enterprise social presence online — *Fast!*

The Social Operating Manual for Enterprises

Everything you need to build your enterprise's social presence online — Fast!

Get *Be a Person - The Social Operating Manual for Enterprises*

More than 400 pages of strategy, tactics, and how-to information you can use to build your online social presence. Purchasing the book also includes:

- Gold access to the Social Media Performance Group online community

- One year of updated information as it becomes available

- Web access to the Enterprise Social Media Framework, which contains more than 50 case studies and dozens of social media best practices

Now taking orders for the print-on-demand or the Kindle version. See bit.ly/gd0FTK for more information.

Visit the

Social Media Hall of Shame!

See rank sock puppetry!!!

Thrill to embarrassing goofs by Oprah and KFC!!!

Gasp at the wrath of the mommie Bloggers!!!

But, seriously, take a tip from Thomas Edison—who said about his attempts to create the light bulb, "I have not failed. I've just found 10,000 ways that won't work"— and check out some of the things not to do with social media.

We include many of the 10,000 social media failures in our Social Media Hall of Shame from organizations who should know better, like Wal-Mart, Nestlé, Motrin, and the US Government.

Help avoid your own moments of shame by visiting the Hall at: bit.ly/HallOfShame

You'll be glad you did!

Made in the USA
Charleston, SC
13 October 2012